Grace Happens

Grace Happens

Stories of Everyday
Encounters with Grace

Bob Libby

COWLEY PUBLICATIONS
Cambridge ◆ Boston
Massachusetts

Published in the United States of America by Cowley Publications, a division of the Society of St. John the Evangelist. No portion of this book may be reproduced, stored in or introduced into a retrieval system, or transmitted, in any form or by any means—including photocopying—without the prior written permission of Cowley Publications, except in the case of brief quotations embodied in critical articles and reviews.

Library of Congress Cataloging-in-Publication Data:
    Libby, Bob, 1930-
    Grace happens: stories of everyday encounters with grace / by Bob Libby
        p.   cm.
    ISBN 1-56101-091-X
    1. Libby, Bob, 1930- . 2. Episcopal Church—Clergy—Biography. 3. Anglican Communion—United States—Clergy—Biography. 4. Grace (Theology).
    5. Christian life—Anecdotes. I. Title.
    BX5995.L44A3 1994
    283'.092—dc20
    [B]   93-49859

Scripture quotations are from the *New Revised Standard Version* of the Bible, © 1989 by the Division of Christian Education of the National Council of the Churches of Christ in the United States of America. The sources for various prayers include: Theodore Parker Ferris, *Prayers* (New York: Seabury, 1981); Pierre Teilhard de Chardin, *On Suffering* (New York: Harper & Row, 1974); Catherine Marshall, ed., *The Prayers of Peter Marshall* (New York: McGraw-Hill, 1949); John B. Coburn, *A Diary of Prayers* (Philadelphia: Westminster Press, 1975); Stephen F. Bayne, Jr., *Now is the Accepted Time* (Cincinnati: Forward Movement, 1983); W. E. B. Du Bois, *Prayers for Dark People* (Amherst: University of Massachusetts Press, 1980); Henri Nouwen, *A Cry for Mercy* (Garden City, N. Y.: Doubleday & Co., 1981); Malcolm Boyd, *Are You Running With Me, Jesus?* (New York: Holt, Rinehart and Winston, 1965); and Avery Brooke, *Plain Prayers in a Complicated World* (Cambridge, Mass.: Cowley Publications, 1993).

The detail of the angel on the cover is taken from Leonardo da Vinci's *Annunciation*, now located in the Uffizi Gallery in Florence. Author photo by Aixo Montero-Green.

The manuscript was edited by Cynthia Shattuck, copyedited and typeset by Vicki Black. Cover design by Vicki Black. This book is printed on recycled, acid-free paper and was produced in the United States of America.

Second Printing

Cowley Publications
28 Temple Place
Boston, Massachusetts 02111

To my wife,
Lynne,
who has been
God's grace to me.

Table of Contents

Acknowledgments

I would like to thank the people of the parishes I have served who have been the instruments of God's grace to me and to so many others, including John Thomson and Virginia Habeeb, who possess the gift of encouragement in great abundance. I especially appreciate the members of my Sunday morning adult Christian education class, who responded to many of my first drafts with love, charity, patience, and helpful suggestions.

The dean, faculty, and student body of the School of Theology of the University of the South became a special means of grace with their invitation to come and be a "fellow-in-residence."

My good friend of many years, John Ratti, has played the role of midwife, mentor, and coach with this book, as he did with its predecessor, *The Forgiveness Book*.

Cynthia Shattuck of Cowley Publications deserves special credit for patience, forbearance, and determination in gently but firmly challenging and encouraging me to do better.

Chapter One

What Am I Doing Here?

An Introduction to Grace

I was in the middle of the Atlanta airport after putting my mother on the plane. I just stood there, staring off into space, thinking about all the things that had happened that day and wondering what the rest of my life would be like.

Out of the corner of my eye, I saw a woman of about forty bearing down on me. She looked as though she knew me, but for the life of me I couldn't come up with a name or recall ever having seen her face. Zoning in on my brand-new clerical collar, she grabbed my arm and asked, "Are you a Catholic priest?"

"I'm an Episcopalian...." I was going to add that I was an Episcopal deacon—in fact, a three-hours-old Episcopal deacon, but she cut me off with, "That's close enough...you'll do just fine."

Her name was Gloria Baxter. Actually, she said, "My name is Gloria and I'm an alcoholic." Gloria had just gotten word that her mother in Memphis had had a stroke and wasn't expected to live, so she rushed to the airport and got the last ticket on the last plane from Atlanta to Memphis on that Saturday evening in June. She had a two-hour wait and she was afraid that she would lose her new-found sobriety right there in the terminal.

We found a quiet corner and sat down. For about thirty minutes Gloria talked non-stop about her life, her marriages, her drinking, and her mother. Then she fell into silence. The airport clock indicated that we still had over an hour to go before flight time when she told me she was having a panic attack. Twice before these attacks had led to a resumption of her drinking. I asked her, "Have you ever had an attack and not lost your sobriety?" She allowed that she had, two or maybe three times.

"What helped you get through the crisis?" I asked in my best pastoral counseling clinical tone of voice. "Saying the rosary" was Gloria's instant comeback. "Well, then," said I, "why don't we say the rosary?" She fished around in her purse and then in a piece of carry-on luggage. No rosary. "I must have left it on the dresser."

I found a strand of red ribbon in a nearby trash basket and improvised. A double knot was an "Our Father" and a single was a "Hail, Mary," or maybe it was the other way around. For those who knew me in seminary, this definitely was not my style of piety, but for the next sixty minutes we sat in the corner "doing our beads." What was a guy like me doing in a situation like this? "Hail, Mary, full of grace...." If my seminary classmates could only see me now! "Our Father, who art in Heaven...." When her flight was announced, I walked Gloria to the gate. She leaned over, gave me a quick kiss on the cheek, and waved the knotted red ribbon as she handed her ticket to the attendant.

I tried to sort through the events of the day as I drove home. It was like a thousand strands of a rope had all come together that day at my ordination as a deacon, a month after finishing seminary. Being a deacon was like being an intern. If I behaved myself, I would be ordained a priest sometime during the next six months to two years. Ten years before, at the age of seventeen, I had come to Atlanta to study architecture at Georgia Tech, but after two years I acknowledged the pull toward the ministry that I had been resisting since early adolescence. I transferred to a liberal arts program and received my degree from Emory University. After graduation, second thoughts about ordination put me in a Marine Corps officers' training program, which gave me three years to think it over and "mature a bit." It also gave me the G. I. Bill to help pay for my seminary education. I'm not sure how much I had matured, but there I was driving out Peachtree Street wearing a clerical collar.

The preacher at my ordination service, Matthew Warren, then headmaster of St. Paul's School in New Hampshire, had talked about grace. He played with the word a lot. He talked about the gracefulness of a ballet dancer, which appeared to be quite effortless but was in fact the result of a natural gift and an exacting discipline. His charge to me was, "God will give you much grace for the exercise of your ministry."

I only vaguely understood what Matt was talking about. It would take a lifetime to discover it and I knew that even then I wouldn't fully comprehend it, but I was aware that something had been given to me at the airport that day. Somehow God had used me to minister to Gloria.

I turned off Peachtree on to Collier Road and headed for my driveway just about the time Gloria's plane must have been landing in Memphis. My five-year-old son John called out, "Hello, Father." It took me a micro-second to compute the fact that he always called me "Dad" or "Daddy." "Father" was his recognition of my new status and the gifts that had been given that day.

Grace! What in heaven's name was Matt Warren talking about? "Grace," said St. Augustine. "If you don't ask me, I know what it is. If you ask me, I don't know." Grace is by definition a gift. For Christians, it is the gift of God's unconditional love expressed fully in the person of Jesus Christ. That much I learned in seminary. But what did it have to do with the lives that people live?

In my office in Key Biscayne hangs a reproduction of Salvador Dali's crucifixion scene, *Christ Over Galilee.* I've always liked it because the viewer is looking down on the figure on the cross, and to me it represented the Father's view of the Son. But a friend ruined it for me when he asked, "Do you think Dali was serious about the crucifixion or was he making fun of it? I mean, look at the figure of Christ—every hair is in place. No nails, no blood, no sweat or tears. The cross isn't even in the ground; it's floating up there in the sky. Was Dali saying that the cross is just an abstract idea that has no base in reality?" Could grace be like that, just an idea floating in space with no basis in reality?

Whatever grace is, it is real. It touches the very heart of God and the core of the human condition. Grace has to do with the Word made flesh that dwelt among us; we beheld his glory, "full of grace and truth." Grace has to do with being born and being born again, with being conceived and with begetting and conceiving. It has to do with growing, succeeding, failing, forgiving and being forgiven, with being and being healed, with living and with dying. It has to do with the presence and the absence of God, with holy history and with human history, with my story and God's story. "Grace is God himself," wrote Evelyn Underhill, "his loving energy at work within his church and within our souls."

In all fairness to my seminary professors, they did teach me that God's grace comes to us through the sacraments, principally baptism and Holy Communion. Confirmation, marriage, reconciliation, healing, and holy orders play an assisting role and provide grace for specific occasions, problems, or commitments. But I never learned that grace happens in all sorts of ordinary circumstances and that God uses all sorts of ordinary agents—people like you, like me—to do his work.

Grace happened to me when I was in the hospital trying to pass a kidney stone, which I am told is as close as a man ever gets to labor pains. I had lots of visitors—my bishop, clergy friends, family, neighbors—but the ones I remember best were part of a small gaggle of teenagers from Episcopal High School, where I was the chaplain. They weren't by any stretch of the imagination the school leaders. Quite the opposite: they were the underachievers and the socially awkward ones who often hung out near the counseling offices because no one else would put up with them. They self-consciously hovered over my head and shoulders, communicating in half-sentences that didn't make a great deal of sense, but they all touched me, patting my hand, my forehead, my shoulder. They giggled, glanced at each other, and then left, tripping over chairs and bumping into tables as they went. There was something very soothing and very healing in their touch, and I understood then what the laying on of hands was all about.

The title for this book was inspired by a T-shirt that my wife and I first saw in the Latin Quarter in New Orleans. It struck us that the Christian community also has a message to deliver, namely, "Grace Happens." The phrase comes into focus when we begin to think about forgiveness. Whenever someone takes the Gospel seriously and asks for forgiveness, receives forgiveness, tries to forgive someone else, forgives themselves, or seeks reconciliation with someone who has been estranged, God enters into the equation and a miracle of healing takes place.

A man I had never met before came up to me on the streets of Key Biscayne. "I read your book on forgiveness," he said. "Since I read it, I've been able to forgive my Uncle George."

"How nice for you, and how nice for your Uncle George," was my reply.

"Oh, Uncle George has been dead for twenty years!" he said with a grin and then moved on. I keep hoping I'll run into him again. I want to hear his story. I want to find out what burden he had been carrying for at least twenty years, and I want to find out what hurt had been released. Maybe someday I'll know the answers, maybe not. What I do know is that something happened to that man and that he was smiling. I suspect that what happened was what we call grace.

Grace happens when forgiveness takes place, but I am also beginning to discover that grace also happens in a great variety of situations. I like to think that forgiveness is grace healing the past, while faith is grace for the present and future. If we define ourselves by who has hurt us or who hates us, we are forever stuck in the time when that hurt first occurred and remain bonded to the person or event that hurt us. Similarly, if we define life solely in terms of economic, political, social, racial, sexual, or psychological forces, then we surrender control of our lives to the blind operation of those forces. But as Christians we are introduced to a whole new set of liberating opportunities through him who entered into human history and has promised that he will be with us always.

This book is an attempt to go beyond forgiveness and point to the reality and abundance of God's grace. The twentieth-century theologian Paul Tillich described one dimension of God's grace in *The Shaking of the Foundations:*

Grace strikes us when we are in great pain and restlessness. It strikes us when we walk through the dark valley of a meaningless and empty life. It strikes us when we feel that our separation is deeper than usual, because we have violated another life, a life which we loved, or from which we were estranged....Sometimes at that moment a wave of light breaks into our darkness, and it as though a voice were saying: "You are accepted. *You are accepted,* accepted by that which is greater than you, and the name of which you do not know. Do not ask for the name now; perhaps you will find it later. Do not try to do anything now; perhaps later you will do much. Do not seek for anything; do not perform anything; do not intend anything. *Simply accept the fact that you are accepted!"* If that happens to us, we experience grace.

William Temple, who was Archbishop of Canterbury during World War II, describes in another way how "grace happens"—or doesn't happen:

When I want to move my hand, it moves. I don't have to stop and think, "How shall I move it?" It happens. But if I find myself to be a selfish kind of person and want to be unselfish, it doesn't happen. Therefore something has to take hold of me from the outside.

On the following pages you will find a collection of short stories about grace in the lives of ordinary and not-so-ordinary people. All are true. Some are stories of forgiveness and reconciliation. Others involve moments of discovery or changed attitudes or direction, times of heroism or unimagined strength, times of healing or quiet times when the Lord was very close. Still others describe graceful lives, lives of commitment and service. The common thread is that in each story some aspect of grace is experienced or discovered.

At the end of each chapter there is a page or two of reflections, along with a short Scripture verse and a prayer. In the concluding chapter, I have tried to outline in simple terms the biblical and Christian understanding of grace in some of its many dimensions. The appendix includes additional prayers, quotations, and Scripture passages about grace.

Read the stories in any order you like. Skip around, if that's your style—each story stands on its own. Read them by yourself, with a friend, or in a group. Read them to your children or your students. But however you read them, take the time to think, reflect, and let each story into your heart. I pray that you will find it a graceful experience.

Chapter Two

The Lady on the Beach

P eople come to the beach for many reasons. They want to get away, to think, to be alone, to find God, to find themselves, to rest. Like the waves that wash its shores, the beach is never still, never empty. Lovers huddle in its dunes. Joggers, paced by the beat of the waves, glide along its edge. Little white crabs emerge from their grainy lairs at night to clean the residue of canine traffic. Easter Christians come to the sunrise service at the beach as if driven by some ancient Druid instinct, await the rising sun, sip their cokes and coffee. Daybreak on the beach also brings surfers, tall gangling youths with brown bodies and golden hair. Like fiddler crabs responding to the pull of the moon, they seem to know when the surf is up. Even in winter they emerge in black, shiny wet suits when the waves are cresting.

"What do you think about when you sit out there, waiting for the perfect wave?" I asked a student at breakfast one morning.

"You think of everything and you think of nothing. After a while you become one with the water. Its rhythms become your rhythms. They say that every seventh wave is a good one and the seven-times-seventh one is really great. After a while you can tell when a big one is coming and you take off. It's kind of like a religious experience," he said, then looked self-conscious and busied himself with his grits.

One category of beach-type I haven't mentioned is the shell collector. They come in all shapes and sizes, all ages and sexes. Shell collecting is a democratic pursuit. No previous experience is required. You can be a generalist, filling your beach cap or shirt with a variety of shells, or you can specialize. Sharks' teeth are popular, angel wings are a rare find, and some say that there is a market for purple shells. This is certainly the case with sand dollars, which come by their name honestly—a perfect one is worth a dollar or more.

After you're on the beach for a while you begin to recognize the regulars. I can't remember when I first met Maggie. She blended in with the sand and surf. You could see her walking along the shore in her white tennis shoes, floppy straw hat, and oversized print dress. She always carried a crumpled brown paper bag that matched the texture and color of her skin. I remember her most vividly at daybreak or in the evening when I went out jogging, but I later discovered that her walks were regulated by the tides, not by the sun or the clock. She came out at low tide when the beach was wide and smooth.

Maggie always walked with her head down. She would stop every now and then and pick something up, examine it, and either discard it or put it in the brown sack. I assumed she was collecting shells. We had a nodding and then a grunting acquaintance for many months before I ventured to ask her what kind of shells she was after.

"Not shells at all," she retorted in an accent more appropriate to Maine than to Florida. No wasted words here. Phrases, not sentences, communicated her purpose and her desire for privacy. "Glass." She threw away a green pebble that had once been a Ballantine beer bottle. "Sharp glass. Cuts the feet. Surfers land on it. It sure ruins their summer."

Maggie moved on about her business. That was all of her world she would let me see, all of herself she would reveal.

It's been a while now since I've seen her. Two summers and a winter, to be exact. The surfers continue to glide in and topple, paddle out, and glide in again.

My wife collects beach glass in a ginger jar. Whenever I jog or walk the beach, I bring her a handful, discarding the sharp ones in the trash as I come in the door. She thinks the pieces of glass are for her, and she's half right. But the sharp ones are for Maggie.

The Lady on the Beach

For Reflection

So whenever you give alms, do not sound a trumpet before you, as the hypocrites do in the synagogues and in the streets, so that they may be praised by others. Truly I tell you, they have received their reward. But when you give alms, do not let your left hand know what your right hand is doing, so that your alms may be done in secret; and your father who sees in secret will reward you.

Matthew 6:2-4

Maimonides, the Jewish rabbi, philosopher, and physician of the Middle Ages, taught that there are eight levels on charity's golden ladder. On the lowest level, alms are requested and granted in full view of an admiring and applauding public. The highest level of charity is achieved when we enable a needy person to provide for his or her own needs without ever knowing that we intervened.

"Grace is care that cares and stoops and rescues," writes John Stott. The lady on the beach is certainly in this tradition, clearing the sand of sharp shells and fragments to save the feet of people she would never know.

This might be a good time to wonder about the quiet people in the world who help us along the way without our ever knowing it. Their efforts on our behalf are certainly a gift, an act of grace.

This also might be a good time to think about the opportunities we ourselves have to become instruments of God's grace in a silent and hidden way. Have there been opportunities in your life when you were able to clear the way for somebody else and to make a quiet difference in his or her life?

It's no use pretending we are somebody else. Use us, Lord, just as we are, when and how you see best.

Stephen F. Bayne

Chapter Three

"It Will Ruin Christmas!"

The Christmas meeting of Al-Anon, a support group for the families of alcoholics, had gathered in one of the classrooms in the Sunday school building, while down in the parish hall the AA group was in full swing. In both rooms horror stories were being shared about the season to be jolly and about Christmases past. For many in Jacksonville the holiday season began with a tailgate party at the Florida-Georgia game on the second weekend in November and continued unabated until Super Bowl Sunday at the end of January. One old-fashioned clinic that catered to the drinking crowd with a "tapering off" program was always booked well in advance for January and February.

When I had first proposed to the vestry of St. Catherine's that we open our doors to these meetings, there had been some resistance and a lively discussion: "Would we be attracting drunks into the neighborhood?" "There already *are* drunks in the neighborhood!"

A month after we agreed to let them in, a stranger wandered into our vestry meeting one night and sat quietly on the sidelines. It was our policy to hold "open" vestry meetings that could be attended by anybody in the parish. I didn't recognize our guest and neither did anyone else, but the business of the evening continued. After about fifteen minutes of routine discussion, our somewhat wobbly guest raised her hand: "I have a question. Is this the AA meeting or what?" We directed her across the courtyard. As our visitor left, one man said, "The interesting thing about all this is that it took her fifteen minutes to realize that our vestry meeting wasn't a meeting of recovering alcoholics!"

Part of the Al-Anon program was to break the unhealthy bonds of what is now known as co-dependency. We had a family in the parish who struggled with those patterns, Chester and Kate, who were on the rectory steps the day we moved in. Chester was a "happy drunk" who was as charming as he could be, while "Poor Kate" was the noble one, doing the best she could through it all. Everybody in the parish and neighborhood felt sorry for her until one day Chester got into an AA program. To everybody's surprise, he stuck with it and stayed sober. Chester became "Wonderful Ches," but "Poor Kate" fell apart and had to be hospitalized.

Another couple in the parish, Harry and Stella, were career navy people. He was a jet pilot stationed at nearby Cecil Field. They were both social drinkers: Happy Hour, cocktail parties, and Bloody Marys at the Sunday morning brunch at the O Club. Wherever they went Stella could always find Harry at the punch bowl, but she didn't remember him ever becoming staggeringly drunk.

The first casuality was their sex life. Home from a party, Harry would collapse onto the bed or fall asleep in the over-stuffed chair in front of the TV. Harry was rather pleasant when he was drinking; it was after the fact that he was on edge, easily distracted, grumpy, irritable. Without realizing it, Stella started helping him out—she made it possible for Harry to continue his destructive pattern. The children were told not to do anything to upset Daddy. Outward appearances were kept up as Stella assumed the role of perfect mother and noble victim, bringing the children to church every Sunday while excuses were made for Harry.

Although she and "Poor Kate" had only a nodding acquaintance, they had much in common in their struggle with co-dependency. At the same time, however, Stella tried several marriage counselors, attended Al-Anon meetings, prayed a lot, and considered divorce. One therapist kept asking her, "Why do you keep covering for him? Why do you put up with all this garbage?"

The crisis came when Harry went up for his annual fitness review. This story took place before the days of interventions, where the alcoholic would be confronted with the consequences of his or her drinking by family and friends and then introduced to a recovery program. The navy's annual fitness review served this purpose—or, to be more precise, Harry's crusty old commanding officer was the answer to a prayer. Matthews had once been one of the navy's rising young stars; at Annapolis he was voted most likely to make admiral, later coming out of the Korean War with a chest full of ribbons. But alcoholism had taken its toll: the navy had grounded him before he became an aviation casualty. "They clipped my wings, but they saved my life and my marriage," he said.

The commander confronted Harry with his unsatisfactory fitness report. Harry's initial reaction was defensive, blaming everybody but himself. Matthews spent four hours with Harry that afternoon. He told him: "I believe that the good Lord issues each one of us a keg of whiskey when we're born. Some of us sip it slowly and it lasts a lifetime. I finished mine off by the time I was thirty-three. Thank God I was able to stop before I destroyed myself and everyone around me."

So Harry entered a detox program, joined AA, and began his twelve steps to recovery, rediscovering his wife and children along the way. Stella also had some work to do. She not only attended Al-Anon meetings, she began to listen to what was being said there.

I would like to end here with "And they lived happily ever after," but life is seldom like that, and Stella and Harry were no exception. Four years later they faced a crisis and it all had to do with a Christmas tree.

One of the great adjustments of Harry and Stella's marriage had been what to do with the Christmas tree: when to put it up and who would do the decorating. For Harry, a southerner, a Christmas tree meant a cedar tree that went up in the living room no later than the tenth of December and came down a day or two after Christmas. But Stella was from Pennsylvania, where a Christmas tree was a spruce, a Blue Spruce if they could afford it, that didn't go up until Christmas Eve. Stella remembered going through the ritual of hanging stockings, putting out milk and cookies for Santa Claus, going off to bed early, hearing lots of commotion during the night, awakening at first light, begging her parents to get out of bed, waiting while her dad went downstairs to check and see if Santa had gone, and then descending the stairs to view the sparkling tree for the very first time on Christmas morning.

So, early in their marriage Stella and Harry had compromised. They bought a live cedar tree on or about the first of December, trimmed it with lights and placed it outside the front door. On Christmas Eve afternoon it came into the living room to be trimmed by children and parents. The gifts were put under the tree late at night and stockings were hung.

"Why is it," Stella mused this particular Christmas Eve, "that you never have enough hooks for the ornaments?" Harry offered to run down to the drugstore before it closed to pick up, as he put it, "a lifetime supply of hooks." Stella busied herself in the kitchen and it wasn't until the street lights came on that she realized that Harry had been gone for more than an hour. By 6:30 her pique had turned to panic. He must have gone by the Pershing Point Bar to wish his old friends a Merry Christmas.

The Pershing Point Bar wasn't exactly a southern version of "Cheers," but it came close. It had a package store and a drive-by window, but the lounge was a place "where everybody knows your name." The bartender had a great memory for names and faces and once you had been there once, he could recall every detail of your life months or even years later. He cultivated the regulars and he had quite a following. When a post-holiday wave of sobriety resolutions reduced the ranks of his clientele, he set up a "Soft Drinks Only" section at the end of the bar, "so that you can still drop by and keep in touch with your friends." It never took long for the "softies," as the non-drinkers were called, to be reintegrated into the ranks of the regulars.

"Three years of sobriety down the drain!" fumed Stella. Rage began to build up in her until she finally ran up the stairs, threw herself on her bed and exploded in tears. "The dirty bastard....He's ruined our Christmas....It's going to be a disaster!" In her imagination she rehearsed the fight that would follow Harry's homecoming: the broken dishes, the children crying, the police arriving.

Stella doesn't remember how long her crying fit lasted, but at some point certain words began to form in her mind. She didn't hear a voice—nothing as dramatic as that—but the words that came to her were something like, "It will ruin Christmas only if you let it." She churned the idea over and over in her mind until finally she dangled her feet over the side of the bed and said, "Oh, what the hell, why not give it a try? What have I got to lose?"

Stella and the children hung the remaining ornaments with paper clips, bobby pins, and string. When the kids asked, "Where is Daddy?" she simply told them, "I don't know." Supper was served, the stockings were hung, and they watched *The Grinch Who Stole Christmas* on TV. After her children went off to bed, Stella placed the presents under the tree and followed shortly after. Somewhere during the night she heard the front door open. But Stella made no attempt to see who it was—she rolled over and went back to sleep.

The Christmas morning ritual came early. The children tore into their presents. Harry moaned on the couch. The children asked, "What's wrong with Daddy?"

"I don't know," said Stella. "Ask him." Breakfast was eaten. The children ran down to the neighbors' to examine their friends' presents. Later in the afternoon Harry phoned his AA sponsor and by evening they had gone off to a meeting together.

For Reflection

"Have you eaten of the tree of which I commanded you not to eat?" The man said, "The woman whom you gave to be with me, she gave me fruit from the tree, and I ate." Then the Lord God said to the woman, "What is this that you have done?" The woman said, "The serpent tricked me, and I ate."

Genesis 3:11a-13

I am always frustrated by the fact that there is only one person in my life that I can control, and that person is me. It frustrates me that I cannot be responsible for the behavior of others, but that I must be responsible for my own behavior. I like to be in charge of everything, so I have to keep reminding myself that there is only one person I can control in any given situation. If I don't put that person—namely, me—under the control of the Holy Spirit, I make a mess of things and, more importantly, keep the grace of God from working in my life.

Stella could not control Harry's drinking, but she could control her own behavior. It was within her power to decide whether or not Harry's drinking would ruin Christmas. So it is with many things in life.

Keeping this in mind, you may want to read through the story again and look for the turning points. What are the actions that enabled grace to happen? The story also has some obstacles to grace—see what you can find.

This might be a good place to remember the Serenity Prayer. It is a prayer used extensively in AA and other Twelve Step programs, but it did not begin there. It is attributed to Reinhold Niebuhr.

God, grant me the serenity to accept the things I cannot change, the courage to change the things I can, and the wisdom to know the difference.

Chapter Four

A Tube of Colgate

"It was the biggest tube of Colgate toothpaste I had ever seen," Hampton Burke told me over a cup of coffee one morning in Key Biscayne. His hands and feet had just been untied, and the cotton bandages and dark glasses removed from his eyes. He found himself standing in a room no larger than ten foot square, which was to be his home, his cell, for what would seem like an eternity. The walls were covered with yellowing copies of the daily newspaper. There was a military cot, a chair, a chamber pot, wash basin and water pitcher, a bar of soap, and an enormous tube of Colgate toothpaste. Then and there he vowed that before the contents of the toothpaste tube were exhausted, he would be a free man.

Hampton Burke was a third-generation Latin American industrialist. His grandfather had been a pioneer and immigrant from England back when Victoria was queen and Britannia ruled the waves. First his grandfather had opened a store, then a factory; now Hampton managed an operation that employed over five hundred local citizens. He was a natural target for the guerrillas, who kept their revolutionary movement financed with a cash flow from kidnappings and robberies.

For this reason Hampton's house was well guarded, but the kidnappers had done their homework. They knew his every move, and one particular night they intercepted his car on a deserted stretch of road near his home. He was forced out of his car at gunpoint.

"They were extremely nervous," he told me. "I was dragged into a delivery truck that contained a coffin. They tied my hands and feet, put dark glasses on me, packed my eyes with cotton, and placed me in the coffin. The lid was only partially closed so that I could get some air. I was given a shot of some sort of tranquilizer, but I never lost consciousness. We drove for about three hours, sometimes on dirt roads and sometimes on city streets. I heard the gates of a warehouse open. After we drove inside, I was taken out of the coffin and then the van, and there I was—staring at this gigantic tube of Colgate toothpaste. I asked them, 'Why am I here? Why have you done this to me?'"

The kidnappers were young men in their teens and twenties, all carrying weapons and wearing black hoods. The spokesman answered, "You are here because of the crimes you and your family have committed against the people, the crimes that the industrialists and capitalists have committed in exploiting the masses. Your family will pay dearly to see you alive." They then named an extremely large sum of money.

After that Hampton did his best to keep track of the days—not an easy task in a room without windows. He gambled on the fact that the guards changed every eight hours. He said that he reached his lowest point somewhere around the sixteenth day. He had fought sleep all the way, trying to stay awake, refusing to lie down, afraid that if he ever lost consciousness he would never wake up alive. His captors filled him with doubts about his family, their loyalty, their love. Would they come through? Would they try to find him? Would they try to rescue him? Would the kidnappers try to capture his wife, his children? For a while he feared they would poison him, but then he realized he was much more useful to them alive than dead.

On what may have been the twenty-second day, Hampton overheard conversations among his kidnappers that led him to believe they were going to move him out into the jungle, where he could be hidden for years. The plan was to drug him, put him back in the coffin with a canister of oxygen, and take him to a train station, shipping him out right under the noses of the local militia. He was afraid of the jungle: "After all, it's the natural habitat of the guerrilla."

Hampton knew he had to act fast. He worked on his plan for hours—or was it only minutes? Pretending to be thirsty, he cried out, "I need something to drink!" That was all they needed to hear. One of the guards leapt up and ran to the adjacent room, returning with a huge glass of liquid. "It had a strong apricot flavor. I took a big gulp, dropped the glass and grabbed my throat and rolled my eyes back in my head as far as they would go. One of the guards snatched off his hood and tried to give me mouth-to-mouth resuscitation. Another yelled, 'I told you not to spike that drink so much!' Within an hour I was being examined by a cardiologist. I continued my act of agony while inside I was roaring with laughter. I answered the doctor's questions vaguely, doing my best to produce symptoms of both a heart attack and poisoning. I was left with a nurse who spoke perfect English and kept placing an oxygen mask over my face."

Hampton knew he had succeeded when he heard them cancel the plans to take him out of the city and speed up the negotiations so that they wouldn't be left with a dead man on their hands. What he didn't know was that a miracle was occurring on the other side of town. A representative of the kidnappers found out who Hampton's personal doctor was, went to his office, entered the waiting room with an armed entourage, and told the doctor, "We've come to talk about Hampton Burke. Are you his doctor? Is it true that he has a heart problem?"

"My doctor is a cool guy. He picked right up on what was going on and began complaining that I was always overweight and out of shape—but would I ever try to get some exercise or take my medication? By that time he had convinced my kidnappers that I was dying."

After that things moved rapidly. Hampton was told that the ransom demand had been met. They placed the dark glasses on him again, packed his eyes with cotton, and placed him back in the coffin, this time with a cylinder of oxygen. They drove him to a desolate park and opened the lid of the coffin. "We're letting you go, but we're not through with you yet." The next voice Hampton heard was that of his doctor. "Hampton, it's me, get in the car!"

They laughed all the way to the hospital, but later they stopped laughing when Hampton realized that one of the high-ranking police officers who debriefed him was aware of details of the captivity that only a double agent could have known. They had infiltrated the local equivalent of the FBI at the highest level and were testing to see if Hampton was going to adhere to the rules and keep quiet about the details of his capture.

During the thirty days in his cell, Hampton was sustained by hope. "My grandfather taught me that *dum spiro spero*— 'while I breathe, I hope.' I wasn't religious at that stage of my life and I walked away from my kidnapping with this incredible hatred and desire for revenge. When you are kidnapped, you feel violated. I acted coolly, but I was filled with anger that I carried with me for many years. Given half a chance, I would have disposed of those men in a very cruel way."

Physically Hampton was free, and his survival of the ordeal was a miracle of grace. But he was not yet free: his rage and sense of violation kept him in captivity to his captors, and it was not until many years later that he was released. One day, while staying in a foreign city, he got up early to watch the sun rise over the tall buildings. "Somehow I sensed that God was speaking to me, telling me that it was time to forgive and let go."

"What about the tube of toothpaste?" I asked him.

"Oh," said Hampton, "that was used up the morning I left the warehouse."

For Reflection

While they were talking and discussing, Jesus himself came near and went with them, but their eyes were kept from recognizing him.

Luke 24:15-16

Not until many years later could Hampton find religious meaning in his experience of being kidnapped. Although as a child sailing a small boat he had reflected on the awesomeness of the sea and the creator who holds everything together, he had no sense of God's presence at the time of his captivity. He was sustained, as he noted, more by the general sense of optimism he inherited from his grandfather than by what he could later identify as God's grace in his life.

The Christian tradition calls grace that goes before, or "precedes," us "prevenient grace." Another way of putting it is that God's love is there, working in our lives, even before we recognize or acknowledge it.

Hampton's story contains a number of such grace-filled moments. Even before he was aware of it, God's grace enabled him to keep his head and be led out of captivity into freedom; his survival was a miracle. But it was years before God's grace brought about a further transformation in his life—the grace he was given to forgive his enemies.

Forgiveness is grace applied to the past, while thanksgiving looks at the past through the eyes of grace. Faith and hope are grace at work in the present and the future. That is why candidates for baptism in the church, after they promise to renounce evil and make a commitment to Jesus Christ, are asked the question, "Do you put your whole trust in his grace and love?"

This might be a good place to reflect on the times that God ministered to you when you were totally unaware of his presence. How often has Jesus drawn near to you and gone beside you, but your eyes were unable to recognize him, like those of the disciples going to Emmaus?

You might also want to reflect on the moments of grace in which forgiveness itself was an issue or when commitment to the Lord on your part opened the door to grace in your life.

Lord, we pray that your grace may always precede and follow us, that we may continually be given to good works; through Jesus Christ our Lord, who lives and reigns with you and the Holy Spirit, one God, now and for ever.

The Book of Common Prayer

Chapter Five

Near Death with Jerry Wayne and Bonnie Sue

There were eighteen of us, spanning five generations, standing in a circle holding hands and praying in the lobby of St. Luke's Hospital, Jacksonville. The whole family lived together, or I should say lived on the same piece of land, in Old Middleburg, Florida. Jerry Wayne, Bonnie Sue, and her parents had bought an old country house before it became fashionable to do that sort of thing. They even operated a small pottery business on the side. Jerry's children and his first grandchild lived there, too; Bonnie Sue's father and mother and her grandmother, Nana Chalmers, went with the territory. Nana's ex-husband, Bonnie Sue's grandfather, lived down the road with his second wife. There was even a step-great-great-grandmother nearby who made the sixth generation, and the local newspaper had a cover story called "Six Generations Attend Family Christening" when the first grandchild was baptized at Good Samaritan Church.

When Bonnie Sue decided to turn her ceramic hobby into a family business, they converted a derelict barn into a pottery factory, invested in molds and a kiln, and enlisted all of the relatives. The women and a few of the older men gathered with coffee cups in one hand and paint brushes in the other to put glaze on the clay that would be fired into floral containers. Nana Chalmers and her descendants would make up silly verses as they went about their work. "Glazes on the vases, and we don't know what to do./Pretty flower pot...pretty flower pot." The finished products, novelty vases, were sold to florists in Clay County and neighboring Jacksonville.

I had not seen Jerry Wayne or Bonnie Sue in church for at least two years, but their daughter Amanda called me thirty minutes before Jerry Wayne's operation at St. Luke's: "Daddy's heart is giving him trouble. They're going to do something with a bubble and see if they can fix it."

I took the backroads across Swimming Pen Creek, Fleming's Island, and Doctor's Inlet, avoiding the traffic jams around the Orange Park Mall. The Buckman Bridge, a three-mile-long span, crossed the St. John's River and landed in Mandarin not far from where Harriett Beecher Stowe once had a winter home. I connected with Interstate 95 heading north and followed the signs that directed traffic to the new Mayo Clinic and St. Luke's Hospital. The trip took twenty-five minutes, something of a local record.

There was a stillness in the lobby when I arrived, like a "freeze-frame" picture on TV. Amanda and Bonnie Sue whispered that the doctor had just left. "They had just put this little balloon into Daddy's arteries to unclog them—they call it angioplasty—when Daddy's heart stopped beating," Amanda told me. "The doctor said this happens a lot and they had a surgical team standing by. They rushed him to the operating room and now they are doing bypass surgery. The doctor said that everything is under control and they should be able to get his heart going again." Then she cried, Bonnie Sue cried, and the other fifteen members of the family followed their example.

I asked the family to form a circle. We prayed for Jerry, for his doctors, and for his family. A prayer came into my head that I have used many times since: "Bless the skill of his doctors. Surround him with the love of his family and lift him up with the prayers of his church." We ended with the Lord's Prayer and then everybody hugged. Before I left the hospital I went to a phone booth and activated the prayer chain at the church, a telephone ministry composed of some twenty or more people who were willing to be called night or day with special prayer requests and then to pass the request along down the line.

His doctors performed a triple bypass and Jerry came through with flying colors. Bonnie Sue was ecstatic when she phoned the news. "Please thank the people at the church and especially the folks on the prayer chain who have been praying for Jerry Wayne." But an hour later she was on the phone again, after she had been allowed in the room with her husband for a few minutes. "When Jerry Wayne gets a little better, he really needs to talk with you."

"Why is that?" I asked her.

"I can't tell you the whole story right now, but Jerry asked me if I had seen you lately, because while he was on the operating table he had a very vivid dream and you were in it. He said, 'It was like I was looking down on you and Father Bob and the whole family. You were all standing in the lobby of the hospital holding hands.'" Later I asked Bonnie Sue if she had told Jerry I had been in the lobby with them, and she said no. Maybe the doctor had mentioned that his pastor was in the lobby praying for him? Bonnie reminded me that the doctor had left the lobby before I arrived.

This was not the first time that I had encountered the near-death, "out-of-body" phenomenon. Back in the sixties a man I knew had been rushed to the emergency room with cardiac arrest. When he told me what happened, he made me promise not to think him crazy and not to repeat our conversation to his wife or doctors. "As the ambulance backed up to the emergency room entrance," he related, "I felt detached from my body. It was as if I were hovering over it in a light blue cloud watching what they were doing to my body. When they brought me into the room they started pounding on my chest. I could see a bald spot on the top of the doctor's head. Then I felt the sharp pain of one of my ribs cracking. My heart must have started up again. Up to that time I had felt no pain or fear."

Little by little stories like this began traveling along the clergy grapevine, things we had never been told in seminary. Then along came the writings of Elisabeth Kübler-Ross and Raymond Moody, and everybody, including the talk-show hosts, was talking about it. I even overheard a conversation recently in a restaurant where a lady was describing her recent heart attack. She said that her heart had stopped for five minutes. A friend asked if she had had an out-of-body experience, but the woman shook her head sadly and her husband added with a straight face, "She wanted to, but the insurance company wouldn't cover it."

Just before Jerry Wayne was released from the hospital he told me his story. He heard the buzzer go off and could tell from the flat line on the monitor that his heart had stopped. "As the light faded, the doctor put his hand on my shoulder. I couldn't see, but I could still hear. He called my name and told me that they were taking me to the operating room, that they couldn't wait. I learned later that at this point they packed me in ice and rushed me into surgery, but I don't remember that. I didn't feel any pain or fear. I was completely at peace.

"Then I was moving along this tunnel-like corridor and up ahead was a bright, warm, soothing light. I wanted to go to this light more than anything I'd ever wanted in my life, but at the same time I was compelled to stop and look around. To my left was my mother and father. Mother died when I was three and Dad was killed in an auto accident when I was in the army. They were holding hands and saying, 'We are here, everything will be all right.' I wanted to go to them, but somehow I couldn't.

"Then I looked to the right, into an area that looked like a room but it was so hazy I couldn't be sure. There in a large circle was my whole family and you, Father Bob, in the middle. You were all praying for me. I was so overwhelmed that I wanted to come over and hug everybody.

"My attention was drawn to the light in the center up ahead. I could see a figure, but not as clearly as the others. The figure was large and had long hair. I believe with all my heart that he was God. He was saying to me, although I could not see his lips move, that I could make a choice between life and death and in life there was still work to be done—I felt so loved. I looked to the left and then to the right. At that moment I chose life over death, knowing that God was in charge of my life and that I had no more fear of death."

Six years after Jerry Wayne's open-heart surgery, he and Bonnie Sue are still living on the same piece of land in Old

Middleburg and they still go to Good Samaritan Church. The family includes eight grandchildren now, two of them living at home, and Nana Chalmers, at ninety-seven, is recovering from a stroke. Everyone takes turns helping her learn how to talk and sing again. The market for Bonnie Sue's ceramics dried up with the recession and the competition from Mexican imports. Jerry Wayne retired from his work as a postal carrier and now has a second, more sedentary career in finance, using his home computer and a telephone.

For Reflection

The dead man came out, his hands and feet bound with strips of cloth, and his face wrapped in a cloth. Jesus said to them, "Unbind him, and let him go."

John 11:44

In the story of the raising of Lazarus in the twelfth chapter of John's gospel, many questions are left unanswered. We are told nothing about Lazarus' four days in the tomb, nor do we hear anything about what he did with the life that was given back to him. But we do know that the gift of life is in the Lord's hands.

Grace is by definition a gift from God. So is life. One could further proclaim that life itself is a form of grace, as well as a great mystery which we embrace, honor, and celebrate.

The Hebrew Scriptures say very little about life after death, concentrating on the value of life here-and-now, and the covenant between the Lord God and his people in this life. The Christian Scriptures, while they proclaim the resurrection to eternal life through the new covenant in Jesus Christ, also give more than equal time to the good news of our God who was and is willing to enter fully into the conditions of human life. That is why Jesus was called Emmanuel, "God is with us."

Sometimes we really don't appreciate the gift of life until we are about to lose it. Sometimes we don't value the gift of the presence of God until we encounter the absence of God.

Grace Happens

You might want to think about the meaning of your own life. Do you see your life as a gift or a burden, or maybe a mixture of the two? Near-death experiences are rare, but most of us have been given a second chance at one time or another. Some good questions to ponder are: If I were given a second chance, what would I do with it? What changes would I make? If I only had a few days left to live, what would I do with them? Who would I want to see, what would I want to say? What grace would I need?

What about the presence of God? Have you known moments when God seemed particularly close? Did you know it at the time or only after the fact? What about God's absence?

Help me, O Lord, to let my old self die, to let die the thousand big and small ways in which I am still building up my false self and trying to cling to my false desires. Let me be reborn in you and see through you the world in the right way, so that all my actions, words, and thoughts can become a hymn of praise to you. I need your loving grace to travel on this hard road that leads to death of my old self and to new life in and for you. I know and trust that this is the real road to freedom.

Henri Nouwen, from *A Cry for Mercy*

Chapter Six

The Right Choice

I n the early 1970s there was a building boom in South Florida. Real estate investment trusts were all the rage, and the most popular vehicle for making money and making it fast was the construction of condominiums. When the bubble burst in 1974, there were more than seventy thousand unsold condos on the market. Caught up in this disaster was a young and upwardly mobile African American couple, Custer and Amelia Nelson. They had two jobs, two cars, and four kids. Custer, who had a business degree, was a construction superintendent; Amelia was an office manager. When both their companies closed down, they thought that it would be just a matter of a few weeks before new opportunities would open up.

Weeks became months; automobiles were repossessed and credit cards canceled. Amelia sought help from the government and spoke with Lynn Ramshaw, a social worker in Hollywood, Florida. But the best Lynn could do was help the Nelsons qualify for food stamps. Even though the family had no income, under Florida law there can be no Aid for Dependent Children if both parents are living at home. Because the Nelson children were not "deprived of the care of one parent," they did not qualify. Amelia left the office that afternoon crying out to Lynn, "I don't know what you expect me to do!"

Lynn remembers with horror reading the headlines two days later: "Man Killed Robbing Convenience Store." The armed robber, a thirty-two-year-old unemployed construction worker, was identified as Custer Nelson, a resident of Broward County. "That afternoon," recounts Lynn, "Amelia Nelson stormed into my office, threw the paper on my desk, and shouted, 'Now am I eligible?'" The incident led Lynn, a graduate of Ohio Wesleyan with a master's degree in social work from Barry University, to begin a search for new answers to the age-old problem of poverty and homelessness.

When I met Lynn, she was standing in the aisle of a storefront church addressing a group of sixth-graders. "Laurence was a young man who was burned to death in A.D. 258 because he was a Christian. Tradition has it that he was placed on a grill over charcoal and barbequed alive." She certainly had the attention of her sixth-grade visitors to St. Laurence Chapel, a day center for the homeless in Pompano Beach, Florida.

"Laurence was a deacon in Rome during the persecutions of the emperor Valerian," she continued. "One of Laurence's jobs was to keep the treasures of the church. When his bishop was arrested and executed, Laurence was given twenty-four hours to collect and hand over the treasures of the church. He sold the sacred vessels and gave the money to the poor. Then he gathered together all the homeless, crippled, and old people he could find and presented his little ragtag band to the tribunal, saying, 'These are the treasures of the church.'"

The sound of a train passing on the tracks outside the door punctuated her remarks as the students tried to absorb what they had just heard. St. Laurence Chapel is located just across South Dixie Highway from the railroad tracks. When the train had passed, Lynn led her visitors into the main room of what had once been a warehouse with the invitation, "Come meet God's treasures. We have up to 115 guests every day."

When Deacon Lynn Ramshaw was shocked into action by the death of Custer Nelson, she was also confronted with the limits of our welfare system. She took the problem to her rector and together they brought it to the church. The initial response was the establishment of a fund to bridge the gap between a family's initial crisis and the ability of the government agencies to respond. The True Fund caught on and Lynn became something of a celebrity in local church circles. Another door opened for her when she saw Gurden Brewster's carving of *The Starving Ethiopian*. She walked away from the sculpture with the question, "How does a starving Ethiopian know that God loves him?" Shortly after that she was invited to Haiti, where, she said, "I could connect with people who have nothing, and do it in the name of Christ."

So there Lynn was, wearing the clerical garb of a deacon, combining her training as a social worker with the biblical tradition of responding to the poor who are always with us. Listening to her speak with joy of "God's treasures," the poor and the homeless, left no question that she had made the right choice for her life's work.

It costs a minimum of two hundred thousand dollars per year to keep the doors of St. Laurence Chapel open, but with the help of volunteers they deliver over half a million dollars worth of services. They decided early on not to receive government funds because that would restrict their religious activity, which includes daily chapel services conducted by ministers of a variety of denominational and cultural backgrounds. The financing of St. Laurence Chapel has become a major element in Lynn's journey in faith.

"When I took over the operation we only had thirty-five dollars," she told me. "I didn't know what to do, but I remember praying, 'Please, Lord, I need a thousand dollars!' People started coming in with bags of money they had collected. It came out to the penny. Before, I didn't like the idea, but now I'm not afraid to ask people for money to do the work. I'm not even afraid to ask God."

When I first entered the office area I was greeted by a business-like secretary with an accent I couldn't quite place, although it had British overtones. It turned out that Judith Kibwika was a political refugee, and her very presence at the center was an answer to some very specific prayers and choices. Judith came from Uganda. Her husband, Bassey, had been employed by the government as a mechanic on the presidential airplane. While he and the plane crew were in the United States on a routine maintenance flight, he was told by fellow crew members that a political coup was imminent and his loyalty to the incumbent president was in question. If he returned to his homeland his life would be in danger, so he called his wife to say he was seeking political asylum in the United States and asked that she and the children join him.

After Judith applied for a passport, her father, an Anglican priest, was murdered in his own home by uniformed officers. His crime was to have been a close personal friend of the former president, Milton Obote. In September of 1991, Judith joined her husband in Pompano Beach, Florida; her children stayed in Africa with their grandmother.

When Bassey and Judith Kibwika ran out of resources, they came to St. Laurence Chapel. Deacon Ramshaw helped where she could and brought Church World Service into the picture to assist them with their own legal status and to obtain immigration permits for their children. Bassey first worked for a retirement community, then for a cab company. He hopes to be able to buy his own cab someday. Judith first came back to St. Laurence as a volunteer but is now a full-time employee.

The cost of flying the four children from Uganda to South Florida was estimated to exceed forty-five hundred dollars. "Whenever we get a problem like that," said Lynn, "we've learned to bring it to God and to the church. We prayed about it a lot and made the choice to send out a letter to our support group. In a week we had over one thousand dollars and four tickets on British Air from Kampala to Miami."

Not all of her prayers end up as success stories. We commiserated over the fact that a former client who had progressed from derelict to trusted co-worker had fallen back into drugs and alcohol. "I choose to believe that God gives us lots of chances. We never, never, never, ever give up. God doesn't." Lynn is still somewhat uncomfortable talking about answers to specific prayer requests. She's a very sophisticated woman and keeps telling me that she simply wasn't trained to think that way.

Her most recent victory started as a major crisis. The Department of Transportation decided to widen South Dixie Highway and therefore condemned her chapel/warehouse. It looked as though she might have to close down the operation. While the surrounding community was receptive to her work, nobody really wanted St. Laurence Chapel to move to their neighborhood. Then she found an abandoned army-navy surplus store in old Pompano across from an antique hotel that dates back to the early railroad boom years. Going through the red tape of purchasing the store, securing building permits for renovation, dealing with the community, and raising the money has led her to become "absolutely dependent on God."

Everything was falling in place when it was suspected that a large fuel storage tank was under the store, which led to the time and expense of an environmental study and a whole new set of bureaucrats. When that happened, she wondered if she was on the right track. "I was driving to a meeting in Miami. I remember very clearly asking God to somehow let me know that we were making the right choice. You probably won't believe this, but in less than a minute I pulled up behind a large meat truck and on the back doors, staring me right in the face, in three-foot-high letters, were the words 'PERFECT CHOICE'!"

The new St. Laurence Chapel will have much more space, including more showers, counseling rooms, washing machines, classrooms, and a nurse's station. It will also have air-conditioning. "It will be cool and clean and roomy. It will give people the privacy they need, help to build their sense of self-worth, and let everyone who comes to us know that we think they have value." And then she added, "We made the right choice!"

For Reflection

You did not choose me but I chose you. And I appointed you to go and bear fruit, fruit that will last, so that the Father will give you whatever you ask in my name. I am giving you these commands so that you may love one another.

John 15:16-17

The idea of "choice" is a powerful concept that lies at the core of all moral and ethical decision-making. It is also at the center of our Christian faith. God takes the initiative and calls us into relationship. We choose to respond or not. God is gracious; he doesn't force himself on anybody. But if we choose to respond to his call, he promises to give us the help that we will need to do the job. The help that he offers is what we call grace.

Grace comes to us in many ways: through Scripture, the Christian community, the sacraments, and prayer. Prayer is especially significant in the process of making choices. Notice how prayer emerges in this story as a major factor in Lynn Ramshaw's choices. Are you willing to pray about the choices you have to make? Archbishop William Temple once said, "When I pray, coincidences happen. When I stop praying, they don't." Others have called such prayerful coincidences "God-incidences." Can the same thing be said of grace?

Does God work through what seem like coincidences or random events? You may want to look back at some of the events or turning-points in your life that seemed like accidents at the time. Can you see grace working through them now? Did they help you to make a choice you needed to make? Does it seem like "the right choice" now?

Lord, why do you call us when you know our sin, our failures, our inadequacy, our vanity, our absurdity, our weakness? When you call us, will you give us the strength to do what you ask?

Malcolm Boyd, from *Are You Running With Me, Jesus?*

Chapter Seven

Bless This House

I first met Michael Ramsey, the former Archbishop of Canterbury, in a helicopter flying over Chicago with Mayor Daley. My assignment was to connect with the Archbishop when his plane from London landed at O'Hare Field and brief him on his American tour. Ramsey had never been in a helicopter before and displayed a childlike joy as our craft bounced over the city. He clapped his hands, laughed, and stuttered, "Oh, loo-look dow-down th-there, there's a t-tr-train!"

The following year he was in New York for a week and we often rode together in his rented limousine. The term "gridlock" may not have entered the American vocabulary until the presidential campaign of 1992, but it was invented on the streets of New York City decades before. We often sat in the car locked in traffic for hours. It was a post-graduate course in theology just to sit next to a man who, in spite of his childlike delight in helicopter rides, had a world-class theological mind.

The Exorcist had just been published and was being made into a movie. Ramsey had not read the book, but he did know something about the subject. "You know," he told me, "in the Church of England, we never throw anything away. We put it up in the attic and every two hundred years or so, we take it down and we dust it off and take a look at it." He went on to say that one custom still remaining from the Middle Ages was the appointment of an exorcist in almost every diocese of the English church. "He's almost always a very seasoned priest, never a young man with ambition or in a position of power, never the heir apparent to the episcopacy. Instead, he is a humble man of God....Yes, a simple, humble man of God."

Ramsey explained that cases of real demon possession were extremely rare, but there did seem to be a call from time to time to cleanse a dwelling or a person from the spiritual malaise left over from some past tragedy. The exorcist simply invites the Lord's love to be present in that house or person, and to ask Christ to drive out anything that is not of him.

I hadn't thought of this conversation in years, not until an early morning phone call brought it all back to me. The call came before seven, as I recall. "I hope I didn't wake you up," said the soft voice of Caroline Handford at the other end of the line. She hadn't. I'd been up for at least an hour, read Morning Prayer, and even done two laps around the block. By then I was into my second cup of coffee and the morning paper.

Caroline's soft voice had an edge to it that morning. "I apologize for calling so early, but Bunny and I had a rough night. In fact, we've been having a rough time since Martin went on deployment and Bunny and I moved into our new house on Parkway Drive."

Martin, Caroline, and Bunny Handford were one of our many navy families at Good Samaritan Church, Orange Park, Florida. Martin was a pilot at the naval air station in Jacksonville. They rented an apartment when they first moved to town and then bought a house in a neighborhood lined with massive live oak trees dripping with Spanish moss. Their two-thousand-square-foot home with three bedrooms, two baths, and a family room was a gem, and they had picked it up at a bargain price. Delays in closing had left Caroline with the job of moving in while Martin was off on six months deployment in the Mediterranean.

"I guess I'm just worn out from the move and all, but I feel I have to talk to someone," she told me. I had a breakfast appointment at eight, but agreed to drop by for coffee before going to my office.

Surrounded by packing boxes, Caroline reported that her daughter Bunny, who was "five-and-a-half-almost-six," had been having nightmares ever since they moved in the week before. "She wakes up crying and sometimes she wets the bed. She wants to crawl in with me at night. I talked with the pediatrician and he says it's the adjustment to the new home and neighborhood. He advised me not to let her sleep in the bed with me as that would cause problems when Martin comes home. His advice was to let her visit for ten or fifteen minutes, reassure her, and then take her back to her own bed."

At this point Bunny slid tentatively into the living room, sucking her thumb and clutching a battered doll. "Look who's come to see our new home!" Caroline urged her daughter. Bunny looked me over—she was not impressed. "Let's show Father Bob your new room." Bunny didn't move. "Come on, Bunny, let's show Father Bob our nice new house." Caroline reached out her hand, but Bunny clutched her doll and went on sucking her thumb.

The tour began in the garage, which contained an old Ford truck with Martin's fishing and hunting gear in the back. There was a new washer and dryer, and stacks of boxes labeled "Martin's Tools—Garage." This was fairly standard equipment for Orange Park—a truck for him, a car for her. In the more upmarket sections of town by the river, driveways would sport a Toyota truck and a Mercedes four-door, but the Handfords were happy with a Ford and a Dodge K-Car.

We went through the kitchen with its beige appliances and on through the other rooms until we ended up in front of one with a big sign on the door: "Bunny's Room." I duly admired her new furniture with its glossy white enamel paint and delicate pink rose appliques. The curtains were pink and white and there was a legion of stuffed animals and dolls grouped on the bed and in the armchair. Bunny's room seemed somewhat cooler than the others, and I suggested that the air-conditioning might need balancing.

"Do you ever do house blessings?" Caroline asked.

"I love to do house blessings," I responded. "We usually combine it with a house-warming and covered-dish party. Everybody in the parish turns out, some guitar players come along, and we go from room to room and read Scripture and say a prayer in each one. We use the dining table for an altar and celebrate Holy Communion. We could plan a wonderful house blessing when Martin comes back from the Med."

"No, I mean now. Could we have a house blessing today with just you and me and Bunny? I really feel uncomfortable in this room. Maybe that would help her sleep." So I agreed to come back that afternoon.

When I got to my office, I looked up the service for blessing a house. The service began:

> Let the mighty power of the Holy God be present in this place to banish from it every unclean spirit, to cleanse it from every residue of evil, and to make it a secure habitation for those who dwell in it; in the Name of Jesus Christ our Lord.

There was the basic idea that I had first heard from the lips of the Archbishop of Canterbury in the back seat of a limousine stuck in traffic in midtown New York. It seems that the concept behind a house blessing and an exorcism are basically the same: cleansing from every evil so that goodness might fill the house or individual.

It was near sundown when I got back to the Handford's home. The three of us went quietly from room to room reading from the Bible and saying the appointed prayers. We heard about Abraham and Sarah, how they opened their house to strangers and entertained the angels of the Lord, and about Mary and Martha's hospitality to Jesus. Bunny said very little during the ceremony, but she was intent on every word.

Our last stop was Bunny's room, with its picture of the Good Shepherd on her wall. We talked about the shepherd taking care of his sheep and guarding them as they slept. Then we said the prayer for a child's room:

> Heavenly Father, your Son our Savior took young children into his arms and blessed them: Embrace the child whose room this is with your unfailing love, protect her from all danger, and bring her in safety to each new day, until she greets with joy the great day of your kingdom; through Jesus Christ our Lord.

When it was all over, we hugged and I went home.

The phone rang the next morning, not quite so early as the day before. It was Caroline. "I just want to thank you for coming by yesterday. Bunny slept through the night....I'll get back to you later." Two weeks later, she called again to say that things were still going well. Then she added, "I was telling my neighbors about the house blessing and one of them said, 'It's a good thing you did that—the last three owners all got divorces!'"

For Reflection

Ask, and it will be given you; search, and you will find; knock, and the door will be opened for you. For everyone who asks receives, and everyone who searches finds, and for everyone who knocks, the door will be opened.

Matthew 7:7-8

A simple working definition of grace is the presence of God's love in any given situation. No evil can stand in the presence and power of God's love, for God's love is stronger than hate or any form of evil. I am not sure what happened at the Handfords'. You could explain it in a number of ways, both psychological and spiritual. Perhaps Bunny was missing her old bedroom, or was distressed at her father's being away from home. Perhaps something had happened in the lives of the previous owners that had not been put to rest. Perhaps it was the air-conditioning. But one thing is sure: after we had invited Christ to be present in every room in that house, Bunny was able to sleep.

Have you ever thought of asking the Lord to be present in your own home, of walking through the rooms one by one and asking his love to so fill them that nothing evil or harmful may dwell there? This is one of the countless ways God's grace will flow toward us, if we will allow it.

Almighty God, the Father of our Lord Jesus Christ, from whom every family in heaven and earth is named, grant you to be strengthened with might by his Holy Spirit, that, Christ dwelling in your hearts by faith, you may be filled with all the fullness of God.

The Book of Common Prayer

Chapter Eight

When One Door Closes

T o the best of my knowledge, there are very few American clergy who have had statues erected in their honor. Martin Luther King, Jr., doesn't have one, and neither does Billy Graham or Billy Sunday. Henry Ward Beecher is memorialized in Brooklyn, while New York's Herald Square has a statue of Father Duffy, the World War I Roman Catholic chaplain to the famed Rainbow Division. And Boston has its statue of Phillips Brooks, long-time rector of Trinity Church, Copley Square and considered one of the greatest preachers of the nineteenth century—although most people remember him best as the author of "O Little Town of Bethlehem."

If you visit Copley Square in the center of Boston, you will see the Victorian neo-classical structure of Trinity Church reflected in the glass wall of the John Hancock building. You will also see outside the church a statue of the stocky preacher. When the memorial was unveiled, it is recorded that the audience at the dedication saw not only the figure of Phillips Brooks, but behind him was a figure of Jesus, larger than life. It was said that whenever you heard Dr. Brooks preach, you saw Christ.

It is hard to believe that such a man should, at the age of twenty, have walked the streets of Boston feeling himself to be a total failure. A graduate of the Boston Latin School and Harvard College, from a family of distinguished academics and founders of schools, a teacher of classics at the Boston Latin School after graduating from Harvard, Phillips Brooks must have appeared to be a successful headmaster in the making.

In Brooks's defense, he was not yet twenty when he started teaching, and had he been left with the ten-year-old boys, he probably would have succeeded. He was transferred, however, to the "third class," a group of older adolescents who had already run off two teachers in as many months. Brooks shared his frustration in a letter to a friend: "I am teaching them French, which they don't, Greek, which they won't, and Virgil, which they can't understand or appreciate. They are the most disagreeable set of creatures that I have ever met."

Phillips Brooks was not the first nor the last to have a teaching career founder on the shoals of discipline. When I was the chaplain at the Episcopal High School in Jacksonville, a visiting and venerable retired headmaster advised our young faculty: "Two elements are absolutely essential to a successful teaching career. Show up for class and keep order. It also helps if you know something about your subject."

To further complicate the problem, Brooks received little help from the headmaster, whose only advice was to thrash them; that was not Phillips Brooks's style, and the students took advantage of his gentle nature. A favorite prank was to pack the class thermometer with snow just before he arrived. The boys would then feign the shivers and ask their instructor to add fuel to the cast-iron stove. When the inside temperature was near the boiling point, the windows would be thrown open and the process reversed.

Another popular diversion was to purchase matches—"of the kind which snapped when stepped upon." A student would cut the heads off the matches and distribute them around the room, even placing a few in strategic positions near the teacher's desk. When Brooks threatened punishment to the next boy who stepped on a match, it often happened that the explosion occurred right under his own shoe.

On another occasion, the boys locked the classroom doors and stuffed the key holes so that it was impossible for Brooks to unlock the doors. He had to let one boy down to the ground through a window and then dispatch him to the janitor's shop for assistance while sheer bedlam reigned inside.

The situation was beyond repair. In a letter dated January 10, 1856, Brooks confided that his standing with the students was one of "deep, steady, honest unpopularity....I would deem it safe first to procure a complete suit of chain armor to be privately worn so that not a heel might be exposed to the assassin's knife of some bloody member of the Third Class of the Public Latin School." On February 7 he was asked to leave the school.

One would think that he might have traded on a family connection or two, moved on to Andover or Exeter, and spent the rest of the school year as a substitute or a tutor, but he saw himself as a failure in the teaching profession. In today's world Brooks would have been diagnosed as clinically depressed and packed off to a therapist. As it was, he stayed in Boston and walked the streets, wandering about the offices and shops keeping a detailed list of all his former classmates at Harvard and what occupation they had found or profession they were pursuing.

The next six months of Phillips Brooks's life is something of a blur, but in the fall he was enrolled in the Seminary of the Protestant Episcopal Church in Alexandria, Virginia. Whatever drew him from the Charles River to the banks of the Potomac is not clear. He did some private tutoring. He wrote many essays on a wide variety of subjects. He had strong views about the abolition of slavery and wondered whether the church and its clergy were not being left behind by the riptide of this great humanitarian movement. Since it was only later in life that he was to keep a journal, his writings only hint at the spiritual struggle that was underway. "The mind that never consciously repeats itself," he observed, "that finds fresh thoughts and feelings always prompted when fresh occasions rise, never having to go back and take old dresses and recut, refit, and make them over to suit new needs, is truly blessed by God."

We do know that he sought advice from his minister, Alexander H. Vinton, rector of St. Paul's Church, Boston, about entering seminary and preparing for the ordained ministry. Brooks left no record of the conversation, but Dr. Vinton later recalled that he had suggested that the young man ought to be confirmed first, and that religious conversion was generally regarded as a prerequisite for confirmation. To this, Brooks replied that he did not know what conversion meant.

What happened in the ensuing conversation is unknown, but Dr. Vinton did recommend Brooks to the seminary and wrote to his parents congratulating them on the answer to their prayers. For Brooks this was a new beginning and a time of inquiry and spiritual awakening, which he would later refer to as "the beginning of my conversion." He wrote to a friend, "Consider me here at the seminary without debating how I got here."

But the night before he left Boston for Virginia, his emerging faith expressed itself in these words:

> As we pass from some experience to some experiment, from a tried to an untried scene of life, it is as when we turn to a new page in a book we have never read before, but whose author we know and love and trust to give us on every page words of counsel and purity and strengthening virtue.

For Reflection

> *Even though I walk through the darkest valley, I fear no evil; for you are with me; your rod and your staff—they comfort me.*
>
> Psalm 23:4

It is easy to see God's hand at work and to have a sense of his grace in action when doors are opening and when new things are happening. It is more difficult to see God's grace in doors that are closing. His biographer saw God's hand not only in Phillips Brooks's decision to go to seminary, but also in his one to leave the Boston Latin School:

> But now on the threshold of his career, he met with failure. So complete it seemed, and so final, that we can only adequately explain the situation by regarding it as some providential interference, which blocked the way and shut him out by some irreversible decree from any further attempt to pursue his favorite vocation.

Grace came to Phillips Brooks through situations and people— the cruelty of schoolboys, the guidance of a man he trusted, the testing of a vocation that could combine his love of learning and his gentle, reflective nature.

Do you have a sense that God has been present in the openings and closings of doors in your life? Try to remember some of those times when God's grace worked through pain, ugliness, and undeserved suffering, as well as challenges and new opportunities. You may discover that your life has been more graceful than you thought.

What is there in suffering that commits me so deeply to you? Why, when you stretched out nets to imprison me, should I have thrilled with greater joy than when you offered me wings? It is because the only element I hanker after in your gifts is the fragrance of your power over me and the touch of your hand upon me.

Pierre Teilhard de Chardin, from *On Suffering*

Chapter Nine

The Lady on the Bus

Back in the late sixties when I worked in New York City, my family and I lived close to Manhattan and the New York airports on Long Island in the village of Douglaston. It was fun being back in the town where I had grown up as a child, and it hadn't changed much in the eighteen years since I had left for college. The Victorian houses were built before the turn of the century, when the North Shore line of the Long Island Railroad had made the old Douglas Estate into a bedroom community for the city fifteen miles to the west.

My children went to the same school and church that I had attended as a child. Occasionally the rector would invite me to celebrate the Eucharist at the altar where I had once served as an acolyte and where I had been confirmed. My sisters had been married there and all four of my grandparents were buried in the church yard. The stained glass windows over the altar were given in memory of my maternal grandmother; the credence table was for my paternal grandfather. Thomas Merton, the famous Trappist monk, had attended Sunday school there with his grandfather, who was the senior warden of the parish. Moving back to Douglaston as an adult was an experience in returning to my roots. Sharing this with my own children gave them a sense of family that they could not have acquired any other way.

My commute to Manhattan usually began with a brisk ten-minute walk to the railroad station, where I would meet a small gaggle of old grammar-school friends on the platform. We would board the 7:19 for the thirty-minute ride to Pennsylvania Station. But one morning in May, for no particular reason, I chose a later hour and another route. I walked one block from my home and boarded the Q12 bus for Flushing, where I would catch an IRT subway for Grand Central Station. It was 9:30 in the morning. I had caught a late flight in from Chicago the night before, so I wasn't expected at the office until noon.

The commuter crowd was already gone and the bus was practically empty. It lurched forward as I selected a seat and buried myself automatically in the *New York Times*. Halfway through the editorial page, I noticed a familiar and rather elegant figure across the aisle. She was wearing dark glasses, a floppy hat, and a graceful, flowing dress, and was sitting next to a young woman in a leather mini-skirt and high vinyl boots who was chewing gum and reading the "Help Wanted" section of the *Daily News*.

The lady smiled and I smiled back. This went on for five minutes with paragraphs from James Reston punctuating the glances. Finally she called across the aisle, "Father Libby?" I nodded and smiled back. Who was she? She took off her dark glasses. "I'm Isabella Hoopes from Zion Church."

"Mrs. Hoopes, I didn't recognize you. You look like a movie star with those dark glasses!" I knew Isabella from the eight o'clock service at Zion-on-the-Hill. She was one of at least a dozen widows attired in tweeds and sensible shoes who could be counted on for the early morning Holy Communion service. She lived on Bay Avenue, just down the street from my father's house. My children went to school with her grandchildren.

As often happens in suburban communities, people are known by the church service they attend, the street they live on, the names of their children and grandchildren, the booth they manage at the church fair. At the same time, whole areas of their lives remain a mystery. Such was the case of Isabella Hoopes. As the bus moved along Northern Boulevard, we made pleasant small talk about the town and the parish. She knew my parents, remembered my grandparents, and asked about the work that I was doing in radio and television. We talked about how the town had changed and how in the days before Hollywood, silent movies had been filmed there. Douglas Fairbanks and Mary Pickford had made a movie at nearby Alley Pond. Walter Houston's family had rented a home near where Isabella lived. Ginger Rogers had owned a house on Little Neck Bay.

The bus ride terminated on Main Street, Flushing near the subway station. As the New York rapid transit system does not lend itself to conversation, ours ended as the doors slid into place. I returned to the *New York Times*. Isabella read a book.

It was a week later that she phoned me in the evening. She reminded me of our encounter on the bus and our chat about the town. "It's so nice to have you back in town and to get caught up on your family after all these years." Then she got to the point of her call. "Do you remember saying that I looked like a movie star? Well, I *am* a movie star." She told me her film credits included *The Boston Strangler* and *The Producers*. On Broadway she had done *Show Boat* and *Wonderful Town*, and for years she had starred in the *Firestone Christmas Special* on television as the gracious grandmother who swept down a grand staircase to welcome her gift-laden family home for the holidays. It was the great American Christmas fantasy, and she pulled it off very well.

"Do you know where I was going when you met me on the bus?" she asked me.

"To New York?" I ventured.

"Of course I was going to New York, but after that I was going to Broadway for an audition. They were auditioning for *Mata Hari*."

There was another pause as I grappled with a mental picture of Mata Hari, the seductive wartime spy recreated by Greta Garbo, with pleasant, grandmotherly Isabella, who had to be close to seventy.

"Oh, I know what you're thinking—that I'm too old to play a role like that. But I wanted to give it a try," she continued. "I *had* to do it. All the way on the subway, I was reading my prayer book and I kept saying, 'Good God, help me!' And you know what? God did help me. Of course I didn't get the part. But they were gracious enough to let me try, and for five minutes I filled the Lunt-Fontaine Theater with beautiful music. I gave the best audition of my life."

Some years later, when I was invited back to Zion Church to preach at the celebration of their one hundred fiftieth year, Isabella told me that she made it back to Broadway one more time. She appeared with Shelly Winters in Paul Zindel's *The Effect of Gamma Gamma Rays on Man in the Moon Marigolds.* Isabella played the part of the old lady boarder. It was a part made to order, she said. She came on stage with the aid of a walker.

For Reflection

For it is as if a man, going on a journey, summoned his slaves and entrusted his property to them; to one he gave five talents, to another two, to another one, to each according to his ability. Then he went away. The one who had received the five talents went off at once and traded with them, and made five more talents. In the same way, the one who had the two talents made two more talents. But the one who had received the one talent went off and dug a hole in the ground and hid his master's money.

Matthew 25:14-18

When I was in my teens and first read the Parable of the Talents, I was convinced it was written exclusively for the young. When I was a school chaplain, hardly a week went by that it did not fit comfortably and naturally into counseling sessions. But I no longer think that the message of this parable is the exclusive property of the young, since it applies just as readily to a midlife crisis or to old age, and it is certainly about what was going on in the life of Isabella Hoopes.

Isabella's story gives new meaning to the phrase "growing old gracefully," for she was a grace-filled person. Her graciousness came from a balance of discipline and freedom. You could see it in her walk and hear it in her voice, but above all it was revealed in the delicate balance between self-confidence and reliance on the "Good God" to help her. No buried talent here. She loved doing what she did.

I was reminded of Isabella when I read in 1992 of the death of the author Isaac Asimov at the age of seventy-five. Shortly before he died, I heard him in a radio interview. Asimov, who had written over five hundred books, was asked what he would do if he were told that he had only one more year to live. "Type faster" was his instant reply.

The Greek word *charis*, which is most often translated in the New Testament as "grace," can also mean "gift." Grace and talent go together. Talent is a gift and so is the ability to use it. Paul Tillich wrote about the "courage to be," which I believe is another way of talking about grace.

After reading Isabella's story you might ask yourself: What is the grace that has been given to me? What are my talents? What are the very special gifts I have been given? How have I used them? How can I use them? Do I have the courage to use them, and to what purpose?

How to make these last days count, God? To live them with courage, and without complaint. To give and receive small joys. To teach the best already learned and to learn a little more.

Avery Brooke, from *Plain Prayers in a Complicated World*

Chapter Ten

On the Avenue
of the Righteous

P resident Bill Clinton participated in the dedication of the Holocaust museum in Washington, D.C., on April 22, 1993. As the first president born after the Holocaust, his very presence was evidence that a major goal of the $168 million project was being realized: the horror of the Holocaust would not be forgotten by future generations. In his address, the president stated that the museum would bind "one of the darkest lessons in history to the hopeful soul of America."

In Jerusalem there exists another memorial to the survivors of the Nazi nightmare, *Yad Vashem*. Included in the Israeli Holocaust center is a street lined with carob trees. It is called the Avenue of the Righteous Gentiles, and the trees, also known as "St. John's Reds," have been planted to honor the gentiles who saved the lives of Jews during that dark period of human history. As of 1990, there were some eighty-six hundred names listed, along with a quotation from the Talmud: "He who saves one life is as if he saves the entire universe." In order to be included, someone must have performed an act in which there was a personal element of danger and which led to the saving of a Jewish life. You won't find the great political and military names of the era; they have their monuments elsewhere. The people memorialized at *Yad Vashem* were just ordinary people who did what they did because it was the moral and decent thing to do.

The largest number of righteous gentiles came from Holland. One was named Corrie Ten Boom. Cornelia "Corrie" Ten

Boom, a Dutch watchmaker, lived in Haarlem with her aged father and younger sister, Betsy. Devout members of the Reformed Church of Holland, the family joined the Dutch Resistance and for more than three years provided shelter for Jews attempting to escape from the Nazi persecution. Corrie was already in her fifties when Germany occupied Holland in 1940.

At first there was little change in the rhythm of the Ten Booms' daily life. They kept the store, repaired watches, and attended church. Corrie taught a Bible class and did volunteer work with retarded children. The only symbol of the Nazi occupation at that time was the banning of radios. The Ten Booms kept one in a secret place and listened to the BBC broadcasts late at night.

When the Germans began arresting their Jewish neighbors, the Ten Booms hid them in the attic of their large four-story house. Through the Resistance underground Corrie managed to collect extra ration books. Secret panels were installed in the back of the linen closet; an alarm system was invented and emergency drills practiced. Sometimes as many as a dozen Jewish refugees were in hiding there and could scramble into the attic within sixty seconds after the alarm was sounded.

The system worked with surprising efficiency until February of 1944, when the hiding place was raided and the Ten Booms and their guests were taken off to prison. Shortly after entering the federal penitentiary at Scheveningen, Corrie's father died and the two sisters were transferred to Ravensbruck in a boxcar. There they had to struggle with the brutality of their guards, the increasing cruelty and selfishness of their fellow prisoners, and their own inner turmoil and fear.

Camp life was a daily struggle for physical survival. Rations consisted of a half-pound of bread and a half-liter of watery soup. When delousing powder was available, the women were forced to strip completely, to the jeers and insults of their male guards. When extra clothing was available, it was dumped in a pile in front of the barracks so that the women could be observed wrestling and fighting over a worn coat or a tattered jacket.

Although vermin, disease, and other indignities were everywhere, some of the prisoners attempted to bring order out of the chaos of camp life. A professor gave lectures. Prisoners played games or sang familiar songs. Corrie and Betsy taught a class with a black market Bible. Still, they have to contend not only with their captors but also with the despair of their fellow prisoners. "If God is love, as you say," shouted one of the inmates, "then he's an impotent lover who either can't or refuses to do anything!" Some simply lapsed into utter mindlessness.

Corrie found herself sinking further into a black hole of hatred for her guards, endlessly fantasizing their destruction and her revenge. Although Corrie was physically the stronger of the two, Betsy had spiritual fortitude: "Don't hate, Corrie, don't give in to hate. We must love our enemies," she counseled her sister. "Jesus is in each one of us, even in this darkness." "I hate—I hate—I hate every Nazi in this place!" shouted Corrie. Then she would pray, "O God, take this hate out of my life and put love in its place. There are so many things I can't understand. O Jesus, don't let me go mad!"

The Allied forces landed in Normandy on June 6, 1944 and began their advance across France. Bits and pieces of news encouraged them to hope that Germany would soon lose the war. Betsy had a dream and reported to her sister, "The Lord told me in my dream that we would both be freed from this place by the end of the year." Betsy's frail health continued to decline and her release from prison was by way of her death. Sometime later, on December 28, 1944, Corrie Ten Boom walked out of the gates of Ravensbruck Prison. She later discovered that her discharge was due to a clerical error and that early the next year women of her age were sent to the gas chambers.

When Betsy spoke with her sister for the last time, she told her, "Suffering does not mean that God has stopped loving us....We must go everywhere. We must tell people that no pit is so deep that He is not deeper still....They will believe us because we have been here."

That is exactly what Corrie did for more than thirty years following World War II: she traveled to some sixty countries and delivered the message, "No pit is so deep, that He is not deeper still." In 1947 she took her gospel back to Germany, speaking in a church basement in Munich. She wanted to bring a message of forgiveness and reconciliation to the land of her former captors.

The horror of the war had created a crisis of faith not only for the victims but also for the perpetrators. The question "How could God allow such a thing to happen?" was accompanied by even harder questions: "How could we have allowed such atrocities to happen? How could our people have done such things?" Corrie's reply was a simple message of forgiveness. "When we confess our sins, God casts them into the deepest ocean, gone forever. And even though I cannot find a Scripture for it, I believe God then places a sign out there that says 'NO FISHING ALLOWED'."

The response of her audience was hard for her to fathom. They were serious and they were silent. After she finished talking, they simply got up and quietly left the room—except for one man. She had noticed him when she first entered the room because he looked familiar. Where had she seen him before? During her talk it finally came to her. He was one of the guards at Ravensbruck—one of the more vicious guards at Ravensbruck—and now he was coming toward her with his hand outstretched.

Corrie knew what she was supposed to do. She had, after all, been talking about forgiveness. She also knew, as she later wrote in *A Tramp for God*, that "those who were able to forgive their former enemies were able also to return to the outside world and rebuild their lives, no matter what the physical scars. Those who nursed their bitterness remained invalids. It was as simple and as horrible as that."

This was Corrie's moment of truth. She felt repulsed by this man, but she also knew that forgiveness is an act of the will and not a matter of the emotions. She prayed silently, "Jesus, help me! I can lift my hand. I can do that much. You supply the feeling."

She forced herself to hold out her hand to the one coming toward her. As she did, she experienced something she had never known before: "An electrical current started in my shoulder, raced down my arm, sprang into our joined hands. And then this healing warmth seemed to flood my whole being, bringing tears to my eyes. 'I forgive you, my brother, with my whole heart.'"

The former guard and the ex-prisoner held hands for a long time. Corrie later said that she had never known God's love as she did at that moment. "I realized that it was not my love. I had tried and did not have the power. It was the power of the Holy Spirit."

For Reflection

Where can I go from your spirit? Or where can I flee from your presence? If I ascend to heaven, you are there; if I make my bed in Sheol, you are there. If I take the wings of the morning and settle at the farthest limits of the sea, even there your hand shall lead me, and your right hand shall hold me fast.

Psalm 139:7-10

The experience of God's grace in dark places is as ancient as the words of this psalm, as contemporary as the stories of Martin Luther King, Jr., and Terry Waite. When I was a young altar boy, I was taught to light the candle on the right hand side of the altar first, "because you always light the Epistle candle first."

"Why don't we light the Gospel candle," I asked, "the one on the left—why don't we light the one on the left first? That's God's candle. Shouldn't it come before man's candle?"

"Because," said the young priest, "God is never without his human witnesses in every generation."

On one level the story of Betsy and Corrie Ten Boom illustrates this truth. They were witnesses and instruments of God's grace at a terrible time in human history, women through whom God's grace reached out to Jewish refugees in Haarlem, preserved some threads of human dignity in Ravensbruck, and brought healing to many in postwar Germany. But they were also recipients of grace. Corrie and Betsy Ten Boom deserve not only a tree on the Avenue of the Righteous, but the gratitude of the Christian family for bearing God's love so gracefully during that dark period of human history. Through their ministry God's grace reached out to the Jewish refugees, preserved some threads of human dignity in Ra-vensbruck, and brought healing and forgiveness to the post-war world.

What do you see as the special moments of grace in this story? This might be a good time to look back over the times of darkness and suffering in your own life and identify some of those events that turned out to be moments of grace, even if they did not seem so at the time.

Take my hand, Lord, and lead me through this day, step by step. Remind me that I cannot do everything I wish, nor do any of it perfectly. Only you are perfect, and only with your help can I do my best. Help me to remember to ask for that help.

Avery Brooke, from *Plain Prayers in a Complicated World*

Chapter Eleven

That Woman in 208

T he elevator was crowded with an assortment of medical personnel along with visiting friends and relatives. A lab technician stood guard over a stainless steel cart carrying test tubes of blood, while a smartly dressed, middle-aged couple carried a ceramic teddy bear stuffed with pink carnations and a metallic balloon that announced, "It's a girl." Their first grandchild? An attractive young woman in a starched white uniform crowned with a nurse's cap exchanged glances with a young man in green surgical gear. An older woman with a bag of knitting, assorted magazines, and a Eugenia Price novel looked like she had come for the day. Everyone except the nurse and resident had their eyes fixed on the floor indicator over the elevator door.

The computer printout at the receptionist's desk in the hospital lobby said that Sally McCart was a member of my parish church, although I couldn't recall ever having seen her before. I stopped at the nurses' station on her floor to verify Sally's room number and check on her condition. When I asked for Sally McCart, there was a moment of awkward silence before the ward secretary responded, "Oh, it's that woman in 208," and then added, "the third door on your right."

The red call-light over the door of 208 was on when I entered the room. "Mrs. McCart? Sally McCart?" I asked as I entered the semi-private room. "Bed by the window," answered the lady sitting closest to the door and surrounded by bouquets of flowers. The curtain between the two patients was drawn.

Sally seemed to be in her mid-fifties. An IV fed clear fluid into her arm. She lay on her bed, staring at the curtain that separated her from her neighbor, her back to the window with its container of homegrown zinnias and a view of palm trees and the river. I started to introduce myself, but she interrupted me: "Where's the damn nurse? I've been ringing the buzzer for fifteen minutes. Nobody comes! I told Frank I want to go to another hospital, but he says that the beds on the cancer wards are all full. I don't believe it! This IV needle's in all wrong and it hurts like hell!" Her whining voice sounded like a long-playing record spinning at 45 rpm.

When I went to the nurses' station to see what I could do, my request was received with less than enthusiasm. The nurses looked at each other and rolled their eyes. The older of the two RN's headed for 208, while a young aide with a southern accent advised me, "Preacher, that woo-man has her light on all the time! All she does is complain and she never stops talking—she has a different complaint and a different roommate every day. Nobody ever visits her except her husband—now there's a saint if I ever saw one."

I met Frank on my next visit. He was a quiet man in his early sixties with a warm smile and a gentle nature. I sensed that he loved Sally very dearly and that he was in great pain over his wife's terminal condition. His weathered hands would clutch and wring an old fishing cap. A package of Bull Durham chewing tobacco protruded from his red and black checkerboard shirt. He was accompanied by his youngest son, Jimmy, a chubby boy in early adolescence who twisted his baseball cap in concert with Frank.

I visited the hospital almost every day and heard Sally air her interminable grievances—not only about the medical service she was getting, but about everything else in her life as well. Frank shouldn't have retired so early, she complained. He could have stayed on in his old job for at least another five or more years, or taken a job in a convenience store or as a security guard. Now all he did was work around the house and in the yard and take Jimmy to ball games and out fishing.

Jimmy, it turned out, wasn't her son but her grandson, born out of wedlock. His natural mother ran off with a Marine before Jimmy was out of diapers and left Frank and Sally to raise him. Actually Frank did most of the parenting, and the two males were inseparable.

Sally's oldest son, Jake, was another cause for complaint. A career army master sergeant, he was married to a Korean woman whom Sally refused to meet, even though they lived with their two children only a few hours' drive away.

I found my own visits with Sally getting shorter and shorter, and more often than not the bed by the door was empty. Several times I offered to bring Sally communion, but the most she would allow was a very brief prayer at the end of my visit. As soon as I said the "Amen" she would pull her hand away and mutter something like, "If there is a God, how come he's been so mean and unfair to me? Why do you bother to pray with me at all?" I was beginning to wonder the same thing myself.

The double-occupancy status of 208 was reestablished when Agnes Whitemarsh, trailed by ribbons of plastic tubing, bottles, bags, and what have you, was wheeled into the room. For several days it did not matter that Sally jabbered on incessantly because Agnes lay there too drugged to notice or to register her own complaints. It was difficult for Sally to find fault with the nursing service then, as someone was almost always in the room tending to her new roommate.

Slowly Agnes began to recover. A great earth mother of a country woman, she was as cheerful as Sally was dour. Occupying not only the same room but the same diagnosis and prognosis, they began to talk to each other about their lives, about their cancer. I even suspect they began to talk to each other about their approaching deaths. Sally still did most of the talking and her voice was still whining and abrasive, but now and then she would listen to Agnes. When I went to their room and offered to say a blessing at the end of our visits, we held hands and made a circle. After the "Amen," for once Sally didn't jerk her hand away or complain.

It was Sally who announced one afternoon that she and Agnes were saying prayers together at night. Whether out of compassion or self-protection, one evening Agnes reached her hand out to Sally: "It's time for us to be quiet now. Let's hold hands and say the Lord's Prayer together, and then we can put all these things that are troubling us in God's hands and let him take care of them for the night."

A few days later Sally said, "Agnes and I were talking about the differences between our two churches and I told her that we took communion a lot, although it's been years since I've been to a service. Didn't you tell me that you could do a service right here in our hospital room?" The next afternoon I unpacked the small silver cup and plate, the little candlesticks, and the miniature cross that my mother had given me as an ordination present. I set them up on a hospital table between the two beds. I shortened the service as much as I could: the gospel, prayers, the offering of bread and wine, and the words Jesus used at the Last Supper. Sally and Agnes looked on, and when we came to the Lord's Prayer, they took each other's hand.

I realized that something was going on when I arrived in room 208 a week later and Sally introduced me to her son Jake, his Korean wife, and their two children. "These are my grandsons, Timothy and Thomas—Tim and Tom," she said with much pride. Agnes smiled and looked on. Two days later Frank brought Jimmy's mother and her Marine husband to room 208. Neighbors, who had been conspicuous by their absence, began to appear regularly. Fresh flowers filled the windowsill. There was laughter in the room, and sometimes silence.

When Sally died, all the broken pieces of her life had been put back together. We had prayed for healing, and we were given one.

For Reflection

Jesus told the woman of Samaria, "Those who drink of the water that I will give will never be thirsty. The water that I will give them will become in them a spring of water gushing up to eternal life." The woman said to him, "Sir, give me this water."

John 4:14-15

All of us have had someone like Sally in our lives, someone who is hard to please, always complaining, never satisfied. It is difficult being around someone like that, and for that matter, I imagine it was not much fun being Sally either. Life just hadn't gone her way. She was like the Samaritan woman who met Jesus at the well, all alone, with a trail of relationships that hadn't worked out the way she wanted them to. Jesus offered her something she had never experienced before—I believe he offered her grace.

The same thing happened in room 208, but we can only speculate as to how it took place. Did Agnes bring something into the room Sally had never known before? Did Agnes' way of reaching out to her awaken something—a need, perhaps a thirst? However it happened, once grace was allowed into Sally's life, nothing was the same again!

You might want to ask yourself: What is the living water that was missing from Sally's life? What is missing from your life? What difference might it make if you were able to drink of that living water yourself?

I do need thee, Lord. I need thee now. I know that I can do without many of the things that once I thought were necessities, but without thee I cannot live, and I dare not die.

Peter Marshall, from *The Prayers of Peter Marshall*

Chapter Twelve

The Philadelphia Story

"**P**lease help me find a parish in a small, quiet, out-of-the-way little town!" Sam Monk had driven all night from Kilgore, Texas to Jackson, Mississippi to see the bishop of Mississippi, John Allin. As he left Kilgore, Sam noticed the oil rigs in the center of town still decorated with Christmas lights and the billboard celebrating the upcoming concert of hometown boy made good, Van Cliburn. The pianist's music would be a far cry from the sounds that would keep Sam awake through the night from the fifty-thousand-watt, all-night channel WLS, the voice of the Loyola University of the South in New Orleans, or the prairie wail from KWCO in Waco, Texas. The long drive, the crisp January air, and the country music gave him a chance to think through what he was doing.

In 1960 Sam was in charge of St. Paul's, Kilgore, a small church in a prosperous East Texas oil town of ten thousand inhabitants. Kilgore was reported to have the highest per-capita income of any community in Texas except for Highland Park near Dallas, its wealth dating back to the discovery of oil ten miles south of town on October 3, 1930. The Daisy Bradford No. 3 tapped into a field that was two hundred forty miles square, the largest ever discovered in the United States.

Sam had brought a quiet style of leadership to Kilgore. St. Paul's quickly went from being half-empty to being full on most Sundays and it graduated from mission status to a fully self-supporting parish. Sam was also a member of the Masonic Lodge, and his great love was working with Demolay, the youth program of Free Masonry. Sam liked Kilgore and Kilgore returned the compliment.

Things changed one Sunday morning when the local sheriff, the Texas Rangers, and the FBI all descended on St. Paul's and put a number of Sam's more prominent parishioners in handcuffs. They were under arrest for directional, or deviational, drilling. According to the news reports, certain operators had drilled slanted wells that enabled them to obtain oil from under properties owned by others. The practice was first developed at Huntington Beach, California, where wells were started on shore and then slanted so that oil could be recovered from a considerable distance out in the Pacific Ocean. In California this was legal; in Kilgore, Texas it was not.

The accused, mostly the smaller operators, were pumping oil from the land of the larger companies. By the end of 1962, 117 slanted wells had been identified and 500 more had been shut down pending investigation. The economic loss to the community was estimated at seventy million dollars, but no price tag could be placed on the negative moral impact. Sam was devastated. Among those indicted were his friends, members of his church, some of his vestrymen, and members of the Masonic Lodge.

The first gray light of a new morning reflected off the waters of the Mississippi River as Sam, driving on U.S. 80, crossed the bridge from Louisiana into Vicksburg, Mississippi. Sam thought about the financial and spiritual collapse of his parish following the legal proceedings. It would take years to rebuild what had been destroyed that day. "Lord," he asked, "please find someone else to do that job! Just let me have a small church in a little town where I can do your work, raise my family, and work with the youth." Bishop Allin appointed Sam as priest-in-charge of St. Francis Episcopal Church in Philadelphia, Mississippi.

Philadelphia, which lay about eighty miles northeast of Jackson, was half the size of Kilgore and not nearly as prosperous. It stood at the intersection of State Roads 21, 16, and 19. The billboards on the outskirts of town proclaimed, *La Wa Chito Aiokpachi*, Choctaw for "Heap Big Welcome," a message inspired by Neshoba County's major tourist attraction, the Choctaw reservation. Neshoba County was tri-racial and its school system was segregated three ways: blacks, whites, and Native Americans.

Philadelphia looked and felt like a quiet town. Sam preached his inaugural sermon, started visiting his new parishioners, was introduced at civic club luncheons, met the other clergy, found the Masonic Lodge, and looked into the possibility of starting a local chapter of Demolay for the young high school students. But these were not quiet times, especially in the deep South. Martin Luther King, Jr., was preaching the black freedom struggle, schools were being integrated, new voters registered, and change was in the air. To speed up the process, freedom riders, first launched by the Congress of Racial Equality in the spring of 1961, were moving through the deep South. To the press and most of the country they were crusaders; to many southern communities, they were outsiders stirring up trouble.

The tranquillity and leisurely pace of Philadelphia was shattered on June 16, 1964 when the Mt. Zion Baptist Church, a center for the voter registration drive and site of a freedom school, was burned to the ground. Three black men were beaten, followed by what the locals called an "invasion" of reporters and civil rights workers. Three civil rights workers who were associated with the Congress of Racial Equality disappeared on June 21. They were Michael Schwerner, twenty-four years old, Andrew Goodman, twenty, both from New York, and James E. Chaney, twenty-one, a black man from Meridian, Mississippi. According to the *New York Times*, Cecil Price, the county's deputy sheriff, heard they were last seen together riding in a car near a burned-out church. Price claimed he arrested Chaney on a speeding charge the Sunday he disappeared and held the two others for investigation, releasing them late that night. They had not been heard from since.

Everyone had a different theory about the disappearance. Sheriff L. A. Rainey was quoted as saying, "If they're in Mississippi, they're just hiding out somewhere and trying to get a lot of publicity out of it, I figure." As investigators dragged lakes and waterways for bodies, a local farmer was quoted in the *New York Times* as saying, "We throw two or three niggers in every year to feed the fish." As for Mississippi's Senator Eastland, he hinted that the three young man had run away voluntarily and that Communists had plotted their disappearance. The governor suggested that they might be in Cuba.

As the ranks of "invaders" increased with the national publicity, local reaction shifted to a cautious and defensive posture. Sam remembers being visited in his home on a Saturday afternoon by two black civil rights workers who planned to come to his church the next day. Was that all right? He cautiously replied, "If you are coming to worship, you are welcome. If you are coming with reporters and TV cameras, you are not." A bold "Of course you're welcome!" would have been better, but that was the best that Sam could do. After all, he had come to Philadelphia because it was a quiet town.

Late one night, Sam was invited to a meeting of community leaders to decide what to do about the new wave of reporters and civil rights workers. All the public lodging facilities were filled and many of the blacks were camping out in old unpainted cabins on the edge of town. The mood of the meeting shifted from defensive to persecuted to mean and angry. Resentment of the outsiders was building. The local leaders saw themselves, and not the missing black men, as the victims. There were comments about getting rid of the troublemakers...raiding the shanty town...torching the buildings. Up to this point Sam had been quiet. After all, he told himself, he was new in town and still didn't understand the local situation. Nonetheless, finally he felt compelled to speak.

Sam was not a tall man, just average in height and weight, and only his clerical collar set him apart from the dozen or more men in the room. Speaking softly and hesitantly, he compared the current meeting to one described in the Book of Acts, where Luke records a gathering in Jerusalem to decide what to do about a particularly disruptive group of apostles. Sam picked up a King James Version of the Bible and began to read from Acts 5:

> Then stood there up one in the council, a Pharisee, named Gamaliel, a doctor of the law, had in reputation among all the

people, and commanded to put the apostles forth a little space;
and said to them, Ye men of Israel, take heed to yourselves
what ye intend to do as touching these men....Refrain from
these men, and let them alone: for if this counsel or this work
be of men, it will come to nought: but if it be of God, ye cannot
overthrow it; lest haply ye be found even to fight against God.

Sam repeated the phrase, "Refrain from these men, and let
them alone," reading the words deliberately and slowly, making eye contact with his fellow townsmen.

When he was finished reading out loud he sat down without comment and fixed his eyes on the printed word as if to
continue his search. Silence followed. One or two began to
form words, but then thought better of it. The plan to torch
the cabins was not mentioned again. Throats were cleared.
One of the civic elders consulted a gold pocket watch and
nodded to the rest. The meeting was adjourned or, more accu-
rately, it dissolved. One by one the participants, leaving by different exits, walked out into the night.

No more violence occurred in Philadelphia, Mississippi. On
August 4 the bodies of Schwerner, Goodman, and Chaney
were found. The FBI, acting on information from a reliable
source, secured a warrant to search a farm three miles south of
town near the county fairground and just off State Road 21. In
101 degree heat, on the Old Jolly Farm of Olen Burrage, a bull-
dozer cut into the twenty-foot bank of a newly constructed
red clay dam and uncovered the decayed bodies of the civil
rights workers. On October 3, the FBI arrested Sheriff Rainey,
Deputy Price, and two other men on charges of "violating the
rights of Negro Citizens." Rainey was acquitted. Price was
found guilty and sentenced to six years in prison.

Little by little things things began to change. In August of
1965, J. C. Spivey became the first black policeman in Neshoba
County and the schools were integrated. Sam Monk continued
to serve at St. Francis until 1975, but his application for membership in the local Masonic Lodge was rejected. He never did
get to work with the Demolay in Philadelphia, Mississippi.

For Reflection

One night the Lord said to Paul in a vision, "Do not be afraid, but speak and do not be silent; for I am with you."

Acts 18:9-10

Ernest Hemingway has been credited with the phrase, "Guts is grace under pressure." This certainly was true in Sam's case—he was a very unlikely hero. He was not a crusader for anything in particular. He just wanted to live out his ministry in a nice quiet town. But when the moment of truth was forced upon him, he was given the grace to say what needed to be said.

In *The Cost of Discipleship*, Dietrich Bonhoeffer wrote:

Costly grace is the treasure hidden in the field; for the sake of it a man will gladly go and sell all that he has....It is the kingly rule of Christ, for whose sake a man will pluck out the eye which causes him to stumble. It is the call of Jesus Christ, at which the disciple leaves his nets and follows him.

Sam also discovered that grace is not cheap. He walked away from the courthouse with his integrity intact, but deep disappointments were in store for him: he was denied entrance to the Masonic Lodge and a chance to work with the youth of the town. Someone once said, "Life is something that happens to us while we're on our way to do something else." That was certainly true in Sam's case—fleeing the collapse of his former parish, he went straight from one moral dilemma into another.

Grace can be something that happens when we are running away. (Remember the Book of Jonah?) Where do you see grace operating in Sam's story? Where do you see grace happening in your story?

O God, we ask thee not to lift us out of life but to prove thy power within it. We ask not for tasks more suited to our strength but for strength adequate to our tasks. Give us the vision that inspires and the grace that endures.

Stephen F. Bayne, from *Now is the Accepted Time*

Chapter Thirteen

Unemployees Anonymous

"It seems like it's just been one damn thing after another since I got here." The words were mine—not uttered from the pulpit, but in a conversation with an old friend as we walked the beach on Key Biscayne, talking about the economy. We were commiserating over the closing of Cecil Field, the naval air station west of Jacksonville, and wondering how it would affect the economy of the community and the life of my old parish, Good Samaritan, Orange Park. Not only did the church have a large number of military personnel as members, it also served a community whose economy was vitally linked to Cecil Field and the carrier base at Mayport.

Miami's economy wasn't all that strong, either. Since I had moved to South Florida in 1990, Eastern Airlines, Pan American, Southeast Bank, and Centrust had all gone bankrupt. Furthermore, I could put names and faces of parishioners with each one of those corporate failures.

We sat on the hull of a derelict rowboat, dangling our feet in the water and talking about what our "new economy" was doing to people. "It used to be that if you had a college degree or learned a trade that you could always get a job," said Clark, "but now we have all kinds of qualified people out of work."

"In Miami," I added, "we have Harvard MBA's who are sending out resumés."

"It sounds like you need to start a chapter of Unemployees Anonymous in Miami," said Clark.

"Is that group still in business?"

"It's busier than ever," replied Clark, "what with today's economy and the closing of Cecil Field and the cutbacks at Independent Life."

Clark's remarks took me back to Jacksonville in the late 1970s. I especially remembered Ben Merchant, a button-down Ivy League type in his forties I ran into at Rotary Club meetings and civic functions. Ben called and wanted to have lunch with me, so we met at the University Club on top of the Gulf Life Building with its panoramic view of the St. John's River winding its way through the metropolitan area.

Over a Caesar salad with crabmeat he unloaded his story, a typical upper-management tale. His firm had been bought out by a conglomerate that was bringing in its own "team." He was to receive a generous settlement—amounting to six months pay—as well as the use of a desk, a telephone, the office copier, and the occasional assistance of a typist. Over coffee Ben recited a long list of corporate achievements. He had been a "winner" ever since he was elected class president in the third grade. Now at forty-two he was numbered with the losers.

Every once in a while someone stopped by our table or waved across the room. It was obvious that no one knew his personal situation, but one friend came close. "Hey, Ben," he said, "I read about the buy-out in the *Wall Street Journal.* How's that going to affect you?" Ben fended him off with a thumbs-up gesture and a quick "Nothing to worry about."

But Ben was worried. "For the first time in my life I'm really scared. Clara and I have just redecorated the house and we have two kids in the Bolles School. The house, the cars, the private schools, these things mean a lot to Clara and me. I'm making a lot of money, but if I miss two paychecks, we'll go under."

As we were saying goodbye, almost as an afterthought, I remembered Unemployees Anonymous. "By the way," I added, "I've been invited to observe a new group that's meeting at the Cathedral Health Center on Thursdays. It's for guys like yourself who are involved in some sort of a job change."

It took some doing, but on Thursday Ben and I showed up together and were ushered into a partitioned-off corner of a cafeteria. There were about twenty men seated around a large table; it could have been a civic club, a board of trustees, or a blue-ribbon committee of community leaders. The common denominator was that three-quarters of them were either out of work or facing the possibility of imminent unemployment. Some called the group the 8.7 Club in honor of the unemployment rate in the community at that time, while others just referred to it as Unemployees Anonymous.

The inspiration for the group came from the Pittsburgh Experiment, which owes its origin to the late Dr. Sam Shoemaker and his ministry in that city. Legend has it that Sam challenged a group of businessmen to pray every day for thirty days about something that deeply affected their lives. When they gathered a month later to share their experiences, each related a unique story of how Christ and God's grace had come into their lives. Discovering the power of prayer, the businessmen began to meet for prayer and mutual support to see what they could do to add spiritual renewal to the urban renewal that was transforming Pittsburgh's center into a "Golden Triangle." As the movement spread, a subgroup addressed itself to the problem of unemployment.

The Jacksonville group simply took the Pittsburgh model and applied it to their own situation. The format was a simple one. The leadership for each meeting rotated each week. Going clockwise around the table, each man was asked to tell in sixty seconds or less what he had been going through during the week and what progress he had made. The second time around each man had an opportunity to offer a short, one-sentence prayer or to simply say "Amen" or "Pass." The meeting adjourned after an hour, but many stayed on to visit one-on-one.

As we went around the table, one man shared the good news that he had been at his new job for two weeks and that things were going well. He had been out of work for almost six months and his new position meant a change of careers after fourteen years at the same job. But, he added, this was probably a good thing: "My family stuck by me and we are a lot closer than before."

Another mentioned he had read that one-half of all unemployed executives end up divorced or with deep psychological problems. A third man had seen statistics indicating that it takes a month of searching for every $10,000-a-year in salary: "A $60,000-a-year man can expect a minimum of six months of looking." After that, a man in a Brooks Brothers suit was embarrassed to say that he had located a new position in two months.

Not all of the members of the group were white-collar workers. One recently reemployed man told how happy he was with his new maintenance job, and he, too, appreciated the tremendous help he had received in the fellowship of the group.

We also talked about what a devastating impact the loss of a job can have on someone's self-image. Charlie, who had only recently moved back into the ranks of the employed and was now a prime mover in the group, said, "Our culture identifies a man's worth with the job he holds. First you ask a man for his name, then you ask him what he does." I asked Charlie whether the group was all-male by accident or design. "Strip a man of his ability to provide for his family, of his self-worth, and he becomes impotent in the marketplace and often in the bedroom as well. It's painful enough to talk about that with another man; I doubt if a mixed group could handle it."

One recently fired man managed, "I'm holding up pretty well. I thank the good Lord for this." An engineer introduced himself as employed, although he had joined the group when he was out of work. He had been on his new assignment for a month. "They just threw me into the job and said, 'Something's wrong. Fix it!' I had gotten stale without knowing it. This is the best thing that has ever happened to me. Every day is a new adventure."

A former middle-manager, unemployed after seventeen years with one company, described tentative plans to open his own business if financing could be found. Another said that he had been jobless four years ago, came down with hives, and took "tons of Librium. This time around I'm making it with the help of this group, my family, prayer and self-examination, trust in God and in my own skills."

Sometimes being in the wrong job or being under-employed can be almost as bad as no job at all. One man said that the Lord was leading him into a decision to start over again on his own. He had just been offered a contract for his services: "I have something they want!" he said with much excitement.

A prosperous older man introduced himself as "employed" but said this hadn't always been the case—during the Depression he was out of work for four years. When I asked him why he put so much time into the group, he cited the rewards of suicides prevented, marriages saved, careers restored, and self-respect renewed. He remembered one man who was so tied up in knots that he couldn't even say "Amen" or "Pass" during the prayer time, but "weeks later he said one of the most beautiful prayers I have ever heard."

At the end of the meeting they prayed for one another. Some said no more than "Amen" or "Thank you" when it was their turn. The meeting adjourned. Some went back to work or out to an interview. The one word that described the meeting to me was "hopeful."

But one glance in Ben's direction convinced me that he was very uncomfortable; it had been a mistake to bring him. When we got outside, he let me know in no uncertain terms that he would not be coming back. "Whatever it is they're selling, I'm not buying." After that disaster, I was surprised that he kept in touch at all, but he called from time to time, and he and Clara even visited church one Sunday.

Ben waited in vain for colleagues and old friends to come through in response to the chatty notes he sent out announcing that he might possibly be available in the near future. In the meantime things were getting difficult at home. If Ben didn't have a plan of attack, his wife Clara did—she was more than willing to give him a running account of the things that he had left undone that he should have done. His puffy face was an outward and visible expression of his inward and spiritual condition. After all, it's not called Southern Comfort for nothing.

One night Clara called me. Ben had disappeared. We decided to hold off calling the police and I contacted Charlie instead. Two days later he called back—he'd found Ben. He wouldn't tell me where Ben was hiding. All I was allowed to do was tell Clara that her husband was safe. A week later Charlie called again. "Tell Clara to get her best negligee and a bathing suit. Ben's out at the beach in an old motel. But tell Clara to give me a call first. She and I need to talk."

It was the following Tuesday that I heard from Ben and Clara. They stopped off at my office on their way home from the beach and I could tell just by looking at them that things were all right.

"Ben has a plan of action all worked out," Clara said. "He's decided that getting a new position is a full-time job in itself. Charlie helped him put his resumé together and work out his strategy." Then Ben chimed in, "And Clara told me that she wanted to be with me—that I was what was important to her, not a big house or a fancy car."

For Reflection

The centurion answered, "Lord, I am not worthy to have you come under my roof; but only speak the word, and my servant will be healed. For I also am a man under authority, with soldiers under me; and I say to one, 'Go,' and he goes, and to another, 'Come,' and he comes...." When Jesus heard him, he was amazed.

Matthew 8:8-10

Being in control of one's own life is to a large extent part and parcel of who we are, or at least who we think we are. We urge our children to take charge of their own lives and to assert themselves: "Don't just let life happen to you." "Get a life." "Plan for the future." "Take control." This is all well and good up to a point, but we are creatures, not gods. We share in the creative process of life, but we are not the Creator.

Sometimes our wish to be in control keeps grace from happening. A crisis like the loss of a job, an accident, major illness, a natural disaster, or the death of a loved one brings us up short and reminds us that all that we are and all that we ever hope to be are gifts from God.

The centurion in Matthew's gospel was someone who was used to being in charge, but he also knew the limits of his own power and came to the point where he had to recognize a higher authority. That is when grace happens—when we turn control of our lives back over to the one who created us and loves us.

Take some time to think about the question of control. Is control a problem for you? Are you trying to do it all yourself? What is keeping you from reaching out for help?

You might also want to reflect on how important community is in allowing grace to happen. Could Ben's comeback have occurred without the love and support of other people? What about the other men who were unemployed? How do you see grace happening in their lives?

Creator, Sustainer, Creator Anew, it is also true of me that my work is mostly who I am. I know myself in my qualifications. I am alive when I am useful, and this morning I have nothing to do.... Sooner rather than later, I pray, help me to see this as a chance to make a worthy change. Give me a glimpse of who I am apart from what I do. And grant me courage I never thought I would need to rise at a reasonable hour and have a good breakfast and bathe.

Robert Jones, from *Prayers for Puppies,*
Aging Autos, Sleepless Nights

Chapter Fourteen

What's Mother Doing Now?

W hile the jury was still out on the Rodney King trial, a dozen women were talking animatedly about the mission they would soon establish in the burned-out South Central section of Los Angeles. They were the Sisters of St. Mary and we were having breakfast following the seven o'clock Eucharist. Outside, a spring storm was watering the daffodils and tossing the dogwood branches about in a wild ballet of white; inside, it was warm and friendly and there was much joy.

I couldn't help comparing this visit to one I had made to the convent back in the mid-1970s. I was pursuing summer graduate studies at the nearby School of Theology at the University of the South, Sewanee, Tennessee, and had agreed to conduct the early morning Eucharist for the sisters, with breakfast afterward. I looked forward to the experience since I had never been in a convent before nor had had any kind of conversation with a nun, Episcopal or otherwise.

None of the sisters fitted the stereotype portrayed in the John Belushi movie, *The Blues Brothers*—they all had radiant faces and appeared to be in their late seventies or early eighties. They reminded me of my grandmother as they shuffled up to the altar rail in their floor-length habits. When it came time for breakfast, the sisters retired behind the closed doors of the refectory while I, "the father," was seated all alone at a small oak table set up in the hall.

Now I was back at Sewanee, the holy mountain, for two weeks as a fellow-in-residence. Since the invitation had come just one week after I had uttered a very public prayer—"O God, I really need to spend some time in a good theological library!"—I considered my fortnight in Appalachia as nothing less than an occasion of actual grace, not to mention divine intervention. When I was first told where I was staying, however, I thought that there had been some mistake. "We've reserved the hermitage out at St. Mary's for you. It's a bit away from the campus, but comfortable and you won't be disturbed."

For the uninitiated, a hermitage is the monastic equivalent of solitary confinement. The idea is to get away from it all, read your Bible, say your prayers, and listen to God. In religious communities with tough disciplines, folks are known to spend thirty days or more a year in solitude. At the Trappist monastery in Conyers, Georgia, where I once stayed, there was an old man who had been in a hermitage on the hill for over forty years. He came down to the community every thirty days or so to attend Mass and pick up new supplies. "We've never gotten around to telling him about Vatican II" was the only comment about his old-fashioned ways.

The hermitage at St. Mary's turned out to be the answer to my prayer. While I had come to study and write, I discovered a white chair on a stone ledge on the side of the mountain where I could sit and read, nap, pray and dream, and listen. I also rediscovered my old friend Madeleine L'Engle Theotisto and the community at St. Mary's Convent just down the lane.

Madeleine and I had first met many years before at an All Saints' Day service at the cathedral in Jacksonville. When we chatted on the church steps, we discovered that we were both there for the same reason: November 1 is our birthday. At the time she was working in Jacksonville at the Cathedral Foundation as an administrative assistant, coordinating the complex of retirement apartments, rehabilitation facilities, and ghetto housing. A native of Florida and cousin to her namesake Madeleine L'Engle, the author, she had been at St. Mark's Church in Van Nuys, California in 1960 when a whole new chapter in the renewal of the church was being written. Dennis Bennett tells that story in *Nine O'Clock in the Morning*.

Although she considered herself a charismatic Christian, Madeleine had never been very outspoken about it, but shared her own pilgrimage quietly with others when it seemed appropriate. She told a reporter for the local paper that "God has always been in my life since I was in my teens. He nudged me along the way and when I dropped out he brought me back. Looking back I can see there have been encounters with God all along the way." Marriage had taken her to South America with her Greek husband, and there she came to a major turning point in her life—faced with a problem that was more than she could bear, she was driven to her knees. The next day, the problem was taken out of her hands and solved.

In Van Nuys, she experienced "the baptism of the Holy Spirit." She puts quotation marks around the phrase because labels mean different things to different people. She is not particularly interested in trying to convince anyone of anything in connection with the event except that it did bring a new dimension to her relationship with God. While in her fifties Madeleine announced that she was being called by God to go back to college and study nursing. When she approached the registrar at the local community college to enroll in the nursing program, however, she was told they were already full and she would have to wait. "I told her that I was too old to wait and that I felt this was what God wanted me to do. She just handed me the form." The next thing Madeleine knew, she was accepted.

The little miracles continued. When money ran low, a check would arrive from somewhere. She graduated in 1975 and began nursing in a local hospital, which she loved: "It is really caring for people. It's an outpouring of God's love through you to someone else." As she experienced the joy of her new vocation, however, she also felt a deep yearning to spend more time "just being with the Lord."

By 1978, she felt a hunger to grow and to serve her Lord in a different way, and it was about that time that she clipped out a newspaper article about a grandmother who had become a nun. The following year found her, with her bishop's blessing, at the Protestant community of Grandchamp near Neuchatel, Switzerland, along with fifty other women from an assortment of Christian traditions. The common language of the community was French, which Madeleine had to master for the occasion. She had a good ear and had learned Spanish in order to live in South America; with God's help she would learn French.

So, depositing the cat in her youngest son's arms and the dog with a lonely neighbor, she took off for Europe asking herself, "What have I done to deserve all this?" In the meantime, her grown children tried to figure out what they were going to say to their friends when they asked, "What's your mother doing now?"

"Oh, just tell them your mother is a nun and see what happens," said Madeleine.

Grandchamp deepened her joy and sense of vocation. "There is much song and joy in living together. I was with them for a year and they taught l'Americaine to love and reverence their way of life. They taught me that we can live together in the love of God, sustaining one another in his charity." When the year ended she knew that she had discovered what God wanted her to be and to do.

So Madeleine L'Engle Theotisto knocked on the door of her new home, St. Mary's, Sewanee. Everybody lent a hand in the housekeeping and gardening chores as well as the daily round of divine offices. Mary Anselm and Mary Demetria kept the bees. Sister Kiara played the piano. In addition, there were outreach programs, retreats, and quiet days. Sister Lucy, the sister-in-charge when Madeleine arrived, had pastoral oversight of a nearby mountain congregation and enlisted others in vacation Bible schools or Sunday school activities.

At first Madeleine worked part-time as a nurse in the county hospital in the valley as an outreach into the community. On occasion, when her ministry to a patient moved beyond medical necessities, she would invite the patient to continue her recovery, both physical and spiritual, at the convent. Now she restricts her nursing to the care of her sisters in the community. In due season she was elected to leadership of the convent, but has now stepped back to second in command. "It doesn't make much difference when the Lord's in charge and you know that you're doing what he wants you to do."

So, there we were having breakfast, twelve sisters and eight guests. Two of the sisters were from the community in the Philippines. The old habits had given way to shorter skirts and more casual attire; heads were not covered, and the women sat at the tables and chatted with the male guests. One of the older women reminisced about the old days when all the priests were men. "We fed you breakfast, but we stuck you out in the hall under the stairs. Do you remember that?"

At the breakfast table there was much talk about the Rodney King trial in Los Angeles and the community they were going to establish in South Central. Sister Madeleine thought her nursing skills would come in handy there and that she ought to brush up on her Spanish.

"What are you going to do in Los Angeles?" I asked.

"We're going to open up a house!" was the chorus of reply.

"What are you going to do when you open the house?"

"God will show us!"

For Reflection

Be imitators of God, as beloved children, and live in love, as Christ loved us and gave himself up for us.

Ephesians 5:1-2

To live in love—to be imitators of God—to give of ourselves as Jesus gave of himself—that is a pretty big order! For Madeleine such a life was possible in community with others, along with a great deal of hard work and personal discipline. Are these the elements that make it possible for grace to happen?

A fellow writer and I were comparing notes about how much hard work is involved in writing a book, and how difficult it is for me to discipline myself to write. "Ah, but it's the discipline that sets you free!" was her reply. Does that tell us something about grace?

In Madeleine's story we also see a strong element of joy and adventure. The sisters of St. Mary's were excited not only about what they were doing, but about what God might have in store for them at the next stage of their life. Do joy and a sense of adventure grow in a community of trust in God and trust in each other? Is this what a graceful life is all about?

Closely allied with freedom and discipline is the idea of self-surrender. It did not take more than a few minutes of coffee and conversation in the convent dining room to convince me that these women had surrendered to the Lord control over their lives. It is not an easy thing to describe, but their joy helped me to see that they had received back something far richer and more exciting than what they had given up.

Take a moment to think about your own life. What does the idea of surrendering your life to God mean to you? Are there small ways in which you feel you are being asked to relinquish control over your life? How would it feel to begin to let go?

O God our Father, let us find grace in thy sight so as to have grace to serve thee acceptably with reverence and godly fear; and further grace not to receive grace in vain, nor to neglect it and fall from it, but to stir it unto the end of our lives; through Jesus Christ our Lord.

Lancelot Andrews

Chapter Fifteen

Create and Make
a New Heart

I pulled my little Buick Skylark as close to the large four-engine jet transport as the Marine guard would allow. A corpsman and a nurse captain waved me on board. It was flight time minus five. Joe was expecting me, they said. They had just strapped him into his medical bunk and his feet stuck out from under the blanket. Joe had lost considerable weight, his skin was gray, and he was having a hard time breathing, but he insisted on introducing me to the only other passenger, a young Marine whose lower body was encased in plaster-of-paris. I gave Joe some get-well cards and a couple of books he had asked for and then we said the Lord's Prayer together.

Standing in front of the operations tower at the naval air station in Jacksonville on this sunny May morning, I watched the Medivac plane, a converted DC-9, taxi down the runway. I waved and then saluted. Noting that it was airborne at 9:51 A.M., I hoped that no one would see the tears on my face. Wondering if I would ever see Joe again, I went into the operations building to look for his wife Jackie, but she had already started home. "It's an old Airdale superstition," she told me later. "Don't ever watch the plane take off. It's bad luck."

Joe was on his way to the veterans' hospital in Richmond, Virginia, where he would be evaluated as a candidate for a heart transplant. A retired navy chief, we all called him Super Chief—at six-foot-two and 230 pounds, he was an impressive figure. His first two heart attacks five years earlier had ended his navy career but otherwise did little to alter the momentum of his life. He was back in college working toward a second career as a safety engineer when the third attack came. At first he thought it was indigestion. Jackie's insistence that he check into the NAS hospital saved his life, and for a week he hovered close to death. When he could be moved he was transferred to facilities in Bethesda, Maryland, where they determined that eighty percent of his heart was dead. A bypass operation would not help. Only a new heart would do.

Joe returned to his home and his church, attending services on Sundays and Wednesday nights in a wheelchair. His weight was dropping, his speech slow and deliberate, but his spirit was cheerful and his attitude optimistic. He became something of a local celebrity and he enjoyed the attention.

Joe and I had many long talks after his return from Bethesda. He was almost too old for a transplant—at that time the cut-off age was fifty, and at forty-nine he was just under the wire. He wondered if he had any right to a heart that might go to a younger man with greater responsibilities than he had.

When Joe and I first met five years earlier, he struck me as a good, decent, practical, get-the-job-done sort of guy, exercising his ministry with a hammer, saw, and paint brush: "Let's cut out the chatter and get the church built!" But now something was going on in Joe's life at a much deeper level. As he learned to pray and read the Bible, he began asking the ultimate questions: What is the meaning and purpose of my life? If I get a new heart and live another five, ten, or twenty years, what will I do with those years?"

While at Bethesda, he told me, a real miracle had taken place. He stopped breathing just before an alert corpsman had stuck his head in the door, and emergency CPR saved his life. Joe remembered little of what went on, but he had the bruised ribs and electrical burns on his chest to remind him that it wasn't a dream. Joe had heard about near-death experiences, but all he reported was, "Before that happened I really was terrified of death, but now I have a real peace about it. I've turned it all over to the Lord and I know that I'm in his hands."

From the hospital in Richmond, Joe kept in touch by phone and by letter. He was twenty-one on the waiting list for a transplant. When Ricky, number nineteen, went in for his operation Joe logged it all in and forwarded this report:

> I'm telling this story as it happens, from a more-or-less ringside seat. The light at the foot of bed twenty-three goes on in the middle of the night. I see Dr. Woods talking to Ricky. I am now wide awake. At 4:30 his wife Rita and her mother show up. At 4:45 the anesthetists show up...last-minute paperwork. Slowly other bedside lights come on, Bibles open, and individual prayers are said. There aren't any atheists on this ward! One by one the old-timers come by to wish the couple luck. At 5:51 the nurse shows up to prep the patient and leaves at 6:17. Wife and mother return for last goodbyes. I have loaned the couple my prayer book to read during the operation. The aircraft is on its way at 6:20 with its very precious cargo. 7:50, the gurney just arrived to take Ricky to the operating room. At 7:58, more prayers. He went in at 8:00. The operation was finished at 12:48 and was successful, needless to say, but everyone went back to their prayers.

Joe was being looked after by the chaplain's staff at the VA Hospital and a local Episcopal priest, but when patient number twenty received his transplant, I felt a real pull to visit Joe in Richmond. The airlines had no direct flights between Jacksonville and Richmond, and they charged a fortune to go through Atlanta or Charlotte. The bus takes forever and the east coast Amtrak dumps you in Richmond at four in the morning. Arrangements with a friend who owned a private plane fell through.

I was about to give up on the project when I spoke to a friend, Joe Gonzales, about it. Gonzales, a chubby sign painter, is known locally as Poppa Joe. He is a good listener, a student of the Bible, and a streetwise counselor, so his studio is seldom without a visitor. "I've been praying about Super Chief a lot. I'd like to drive up with you." So Poppa Joe Gonzales and I got ourselves organized and headed out to I-95 the next morning at 6:00 A.M., pulling into the VA Hospital parking lot at 6:30 that evening.

Joe was expecting us and greeted me with a tired but cheerful, "How's it going, Friar Tuck?" We spent the evening and the better part of the next day with Joe in the open cardiac ward in an old barracks-type military hospital with eighteen beds. At first I wondered how a forty-year-old building could possibly accommodate or support state-of-the-art medical technology, but there is more to medicine than hardware. There existed among those eighteen men a fellowship and a community that would have been lost in a cluster of private rooms. It was a healing community and Joe was its spiritual leader and unofficial chaplain.

We were in a new world, one that I had heard about but never really knew existed. We had lunch with a thirty-two-year-old man who had the build and feistiness of a boxer. He was going home to Texas the next day. He had his first coronary at the age of twenty-two, and ninety days ago he had received his new heart. He was to report back every six weeks for a year; in the meantime he would be working on his master's degree.

I asked where donated hearts came from and someone showed me a UPI news clipping datelined Miami that told of a local eighteen-year-old's heart being removed after a fatal accident on the Florida Turnpike and transplanted into a fifty-year-old man at the Medical College of Virginia. His kidneys went to Houston. "They're trying to discourage that kind of information," Joe said, "because some freaky things have been happening. The parents of one donor traced their daughter's heart to a young recipient and started sending presents."

We ended our two-day visit with Holy Communion. Joe Mayers, a licensed lay reader, read one of the lessons. Joe Gonzales read another and added to the prayers of intercession. After the Eucharist, we laid hands on Joe and prayed for his recovery. The words of Psalm 51 came to mind: "Create in me a clean heart, O God, and renew a right spirit within me."

Joe's vital statistics went into the computer the following weekend, while his wife Jackie arrived in Richmond and settled into a nearby motel to wait and watch. The first heart matched Joe's needs in every way except it was too small. A second came on line only to reveal an undiagnosed congenital defect. A third followed but did not match all his specifications. Jackie helped teach ceramics in the occupational therapy unit. The folks at Good Samaritan continued to pray.

Joe continued to minister to his fellow patients, but after the third false alarm, his condition began to go downhill. He was placed in a private room where there would be less noise. But when one of his ward mates was heading down the hall for bypass surgery, Joe caught up with him in his wheelchair to wish him well and offer a prayer. Then he rolled down to the surgical waiting room to leave his prayer book with the patient's wife.

And then it happened. At four o'clock on Wednesday afternoon, July 13, the alert went out. A heart matching Joe's requirements had come on the computer. At six the organ transplant team car left the hospital with sirens blaring, heading for the airport and a city some four hundred miles away.

Word spread quickly at Good Samaritan, and a larger-than-usual crowd turned up at the Wednesday evening Eucharist and Healing Service. It was dedicated to Joe's operation. About the time we were receiving communion, Joe was being prepped. He was rolled into the surgical suite at 10 P.M., and at 3:30 the next morning the operation was complete. Joe had a new heart. "It was a textbook case," reported the chaplain. "His new heart started beating right off."

Five days after the operation Jackie wrote to us:

> I can dress in jeans and go in with Joe. I am running the EKG machine and learning about his medicines and what they're for. I even got Joe's pulse right the first time. (Who says you can't teach an old Airdale new tricks?)
>
> Joe is starting to do fine. He no longer imagines things. Yesterday he said that Jesus was holding him in his arms and another time the Virgin Mary was watching over him. He has gotten over his crying spells. The nurse says this is normal after surgery....P.S. If the TV stations call don't tell them anything.

About a month after the operation Joe placed a prearranged collect call from a pay phone on the ward. I recorded the call and played it for the congregation that Wednesday night. Joe was somewhat short of breath but his personality and spirit came through loud and clear. "I just want to thank you guys for all your love and prayers. I wanna thank that kid who got run over by a tractor for my new heart and I wanna thank the good Lord...." He choked up at this point.

On Saturday night a call came from Jackie just before I turned out my light. "Please say some special prayers for Joe at the service tomorrow. He's running a fever." Jackie was matter-of-fact about the whole thing, but when she called again at two that morning, it was a different story. Joe's fever was up to 104 and he was going into convulsions. "The doctors say he is rejecting his heart."

We had a prayer chain at Good Samaritan made up mainly of women. There were about twenty-four names on the list—some were marked "daytime only," others could be called at any time. I looked at my watch and hesitated. It was now 2:30 A.M., but if there was ever a time to use the prayer chain in the middle of the night, this was it.

A larger-than-normal congregation gathered at the early service. The phone in the kitchen rang just as we were finishing the announcements and one of the ushers answered. I stopped talking as we all waited for the announcement that we feared. When the usher, also a navy chief, returned it was obvious what the message was. He managed, "It was the chaplain. Joe died about an hour ago."

When time came for the Eucharist, the bread and wine were placed on the altar in silence. "All things come of thee, O Lord, and of thine own have we given thee."

The next words I said to the congregation were "Lift up your hearts," and all I could think of was Joe's heart. The congregation responded, "We lift them up to the Lord."

I came back with, "Let us give thanks to the Lord our God." How could we give thanks when Joe was dead? "It is right to give him thanks and praise." Why was it right? How could we find God's grace in any of this?

"Therefore we praise you, joining our voices with angels and archangels and with all the company of heaven, who forever sing this hymn to proclaim the glory of your name: 'Holy, holy, holy....'"

For Reflection

To you, O Lord, I call; my rock, do not refuse to hear me, for if you are silent to me, I shall be like those who go down to the Pit. Hear the voice of my supplication, as I cry to you for help, as I lift up my hands toward your most holy sanctuary.

Psalm 28:1-2

Joe's death created a crisis of faith for our whole congregation. We had all made a tremendous investment in the success of his heart transplant. Where was God in all of this? We wanted him to say yes and he said no. Was God's grace in the no?

Several years later when a second member of our congregation went off to Richmond for a heart transplant, which was a complete success, people were more guarded. To pray for someone or something involves a risk. It involves being vulnerable. No one wants to get hurt and no one wants to look stupid. A friend of mine says that it is easy to see God's grace in the good things that happen to us. It is more difficult to see his grace in the painful and the disappointing.

Prayer is not magic; it's a mystery. Grace, too, is a mystery. If we think of grace as success in human terms, then we are bound to be disappointed. If, on the other hand, we see grace as God's presence in any situation, even something as horrible as the cross, then we are open to a whole new set of possibilities. This might be a good time to think of some of the pain that has come your way, and the different ways God's grace has been revealed through it.

God to enfold me, God to surround me,
God in my speaking, God in my thinking.
God in my sleeping, God in my waking,

God in my watching, God in my hoping.
God in my life, God in my lips,
God in my soul, God in my heart.
God in my suffering, God in my slumber,
God in mine ever-living soul, God in my eternity.

Celtic Prayer

Chapter Sixteen

Class Reunion

T here were not many people in church on that July Sunday morning, so right away I spotted the visiting family taking up two whole rows. There was no question that there was a blood line running straight through the group. It would have been an interesting study in genetics to see the dominant traits of the matriarch and patriarch reproduced in the faces of the assembled children and grandchildren. The grandfather had a chubby face and an infectious, ear-to-ear grin. The grandmother's face was almond-shaped, with a tiny rosebud mouth and large, sparkling, round eyes. I knew that smile and those eyes from somewhere...but where?

I had a sermon to preach and a service to conduct, so I couldn't just stand there in the chancel staring at rows eight and nine on the right-hand side. I put the question on the back burner—or into that auxiliary computer where my memory bank is searched. Right away I realized I was developing a strong craving for chocolate, and by the time we sang the closing hymn I was certain they were a navy family I knew from St. Catherine's, Jacksonville. I still wanted some chocolate, but what were their names?

"You probably don't remember us," said the grandmother. "We're the Wilcoxes. You knew us in Jacksonville. We were in the Navy: Margaret and Morgan. They used to call us the M & M's."

Introductions of children and grandchildren, sons-in-law and daughters-in-law followed. There were eighteen of them altogether. Margaret and Morgan were celebrating their fortieth wedding anniversary and they had all booked space on an overnight cruise to the Bahamas. They had heard that I was on

Key Biscayne and thought they would "just pop by to say hello."

As we parted company in the parking lot, Margaret sent me a coded message. "You know we were transferred to Norfolk shortly after I attended the fifteenth reunion of my graduation from Roosevelt High." She winked, blew me a kiss, and got into a van jammed with grandchildren.

Yes, I remembered the M & M's! They were a good, decent family who were in church almost every Sunday. And yes, I remembered the Roosevelt High School reunion. The Jacksonville newspapers gave it a lot of coverage because many of the graduates were still in the community and many more were coming back for the occasion.

The M & M's were not in church on the Sunday following the big dance at the old Mayflower Hotel, but this neither surprised nor worried me. Either they had stayed out late and slept in or they had joined the crowd at a downtown church who advertised a special service called "Honoring the Class of '48" and brought in a popular member of that class to be the featured preacher. "No sense trying to compete with that" was the sage advice of my senior warden.

A week later, however, only Morgan and the children were in church. "Margaret's taken the day off. She's really worn out from that reunion." Several weeks went by before I saw Margaret again. She asked if she could stop by my office in the late afternoon on her way home from work.

"I guess you've been wondering why I haven't been in church for a month." Before I could respond, she continued, "I've been wondering, too. You see, something happened at the class reunion. Oh, I haven't committed any big sin or had an affair or anything like that, but I'm all torn up inside and I just can't face going up for communion with Morgan when I'm feeling the things that I'm feeling. Morgan's such a good and decent man. This shouldn't be happening."

Margaret went on to tell me that she had run into an old friend, let's call him Neal, at the reunion. "He wasn't even an old boyfriend—just a guy I knew and worked with on the school paper. We found out that our offices are right around the corner from each other and we agreed to meet for coffee. Sometimes we have lunch together, nothing special, nothing fancy, just a sandwich. We go dutch, pay our own way.

"Nothing has happened between us. I won't even let him light my cigarette. But I know something's happening—we talk all the time, we're interested in so many of the same things. He works for the paper and keeps meeting all kinds of interesting people. He was in Miami during the Cuban Missile Crisis and is doing research on the influx of Cuban refugees into South Florida. Neal keeps asking me about my writing—he remembers the sort of thing I used to do on the school paper and he thinks I ought to try my hand at it again."

Margaret started to sniffle. I reached for the Kleenex. The sniffle became a cry and then a sob. "He's so interesting and so exciting and I feel so alive when I'm with him....I'm falling in love. I don't have any business falling in love. I'm a married woman with two children. I'm married to a good and decent man—good and decent and dull. And don't tell me what my Christian duty is. I know what my Christian duty is." More sobbing and more Kleenex.

Margaret and I continued to meet about once a week and Margaret and Neal continued to meet almost every day. The parameters of the discussions had been established at that first meeting. Margaret's head was in one place, her heart in another. She knew what she ought to do and she knew what she wanted to do. In the meantime, her encounters with Neal were moving slowly but surely in the direction of an affair. A quick drink after work became an early supper, which turned into a leisurely dinner under the pretext of "working late to get those special reports done." Still there was "nothing physical," but she kept coming to talk.

My offer to pray with her was rejected as too manipulative: "I already know what God has to say about all this." Sometimes I was able to focus the conversation on her children, her home, occasionally on Morgan. They hadn't made love since the class reunion; she told him she needed to have her birth control pills checked out. In our talks, Morgan was always "that decent man...a bit dull, but good and decent."

The inevitable crisis came when Morgan's squadron was off on a weekend exercise. Their son was away on a camping trip and their daughter had been invited to her first slumber party. Margaret told me over the phone that Neal wanted her to meet him down at St. Augustine Beach for dinner.

"That's forty miles south of here," I said.

"I know that," she said, "and I know that he's not going to want to come back until the morning. I know what this means and I don't know how it's going to come out. Pray for me."

I wish I could tell you about the candlelight conversation muted by the sound of the surf, but I can't. All I know is that Margaret was in church the next Sunday with Morgan and the children. She looked terrible, but she took communion with her family. Six months later she and Morgan told me that they were being transferred to the Norfolk area and she was three months pregnant. She gave me a hug and said goodbye.

For Reflection

For I do not do what I want, but I do the very thing I hate. Now if I do what I do not want, I agree that the law is good. But in fact it is no longer I that do it, but sin that dwells within me.

Romans 7:15-17

It was very gracious of Margaret to bring Morgan and their children and grandchildren by the church to see me and let me know that it had turned out well for them. I believed at the time that Margaret had made the right decision, but you never know how things will turn out.

At the time that I knew the M & M's, I had not heard the phrase, "Love is a decision, not a feeling." Margaret was not the first person to discover that her head was in one place and her heart in another. It happened to St. Paul and it happens to me all the time. It takes a lot of grace sometimes to "do the right thing."

Part of maturing as a Christian is learning to trust that the grace available in the past will be there for us today and again tomorrow. That may be what the Lord had in mind when he taught us to pray, "Give us this day our daily bread."

When I think about the M & M's I realize that adultery is just as likely to begin with friendship as with sex. What was it that drew Margaret to Neal? What was missing in her relationship with her husband that she found in rediscovering her old acquaintance from high school? Infidelity that begins on the level of sexual attraction is well documented, and in some ways it is easier to deal with. Male-female bonding that begins with friendship and mutual interest can be just as destructive of a marriage and is not as easily handled.

In thinking about this story, here are some questions you might want to ask yourself. With whom do you identify in this story? Have there been times in your life when your feelings were in one place and your mind in another? Is this what temptation is all about? Have you ever had to make a decision like the one Margaret made, and did you sense the presence of God's grace as you made it? Or do you sense it now, long afterward?

You are our life and light. You are our journey and our home. In your presence now we ask for nothing save you and your Spirit—great, gentle, persistent in your love for us. Glory be to you—God of grace and God of glory.

John B. Coburn, from *A Diary of Prayers*

Chapter Seventeen

The Good News Bears

T hey were as diverse a collection of pre-adolescent boys as you would find anywhere, most of them answered to "Bubba," and they were going to be my roommates for the next ten days. When I agreed to help out at Camp Weed that summer, I had no idea that I would actually have to sleep in a cabin with the campers.

In the past, the clergy at Camp Weed had served as chaplains and teachers. We were expected to take our turn conducting services, teach a Bible class in the morning, show up for meals and be friendly to the campers, keep an eye on the counselors, and help where needed. The rest of the time we would be free to catch up on our reading, sailing, fishing, or all three.

It was the ambiguous and undefined "help where needed" clause that had placed me in the west wing of the cabin. It hadn't been planned that way—the camp director had boasted of "a first-class team of college students" who would serve as the staff for that summer. One sophomore from the University of Florida never showed up. A football player who was to have been the athletic director had been taken by helicopter to Tallahassee for an emergency appendectomy. Then there was the co-ed and the jock from Florida State who had been asked to leave. That left the sixth, seventh, and eighth grade camp short four cabin counselors.

Father Charlie, the camp director, tried to present the problem as a great opportunity for us clergy types to have "a significant, hands-on experience" with the youth of the church. That was how he talked. Rooming with the boys would also give us a chance to hone our counseling and Christian education skills. "Besides," said Father Charlie, "I don't know what else we're going to do other than send them home and refund their money." Reluctantly, we all agreed to do the best we could. But what about the campers?

"They didn't tell me I was going to have to sleep with a priest," complained an anonymous voice from the community bathroom.

"Keep your voice down," advised another. "He might hear you."

"Oh, he's probably deaf!" announced a third, followed by a peal of laughter. I could tell it was going to be a challenging week.

By common consent campers were to return to their cabins by 9:30 P.M. and get ready for bed. From 10:00 to 10:30 we were to have "time for reflection," which meant going over the events of the day and then having a prayer before lights out. We spent the first evening getting acquainted, telling where we were from, what sports we liked, what our favorite TV shows were. We concluded with the Lord's Prayer and turned off the lights.

Someone whose favorite show was *The Waltons* started a chain reaction: "Good night, John-boy...good night, Barry...good night, Allen...good night, Billy Bob...good night, Father Bob...." I tried to go to sleep, but the more I tried, the more awake I became.

Then I heard someone's bed creak and bare feet hitting the floor. I assumed that it was one of the kids heading for the bathroom. Then I heard a whisper, "I think he's gone to sleep." Other beds creaked and there were more feet on the floor. I listened intently. About half of them were doing something with the blankets. Some weak streaks of light were bouncing off the ceiling.

I very carefully turned my head on the pillow. They had made a tent with the blankets over two of the beds. Five or six of them were on the floor with flashlights under the blankets and sounds of amazement and wonder leaked out with the streaks of light. "Wow! Look at those!"..."She looks like the history teacher!"…"Nah, she looks like your big sister—and I do mean your *big* sister!"

It didn't take long to figure out what they were up to. I walked quietly over and pulled the blanket off with one hand and confiscated the copy of *Playboy* with the other. Pandemonium reigned for the thirty seconds it took for the boys to scramble back to their beds and feign sleep. Everyone made it except for Bubba George from Lake City, whose blanket was still in my hand. It didn't seem fair to single out George for what had been a corporate endeavor, so I handed him his blanket and said, "Everybody go to sleep. We'll deal with this tomorrow." I wanted to add, "Pleasant dreams," but thought better of it.

Over coffee with the staff the next morning I discovered that my cabin wasn't the only one to have trouble getting to sleep, nor the only one to have sex as the major topic of discussion. The camp nurse found her girls in the shower room at midnight trading pictures of boyfriends. Another priest was awakened by a gaggle of eighth-grade boys who were tiptoeing out to raid one of the girls' cabins.

"Let's all look at this as an opportunity to do some significant teaching," declared Father Charlie, before outlining a full day's activities that included Bible study, swimming and waterfront safety, arts and crafts, folk dancing in the evening, and organizing the Camp Weed softball league. He also mentioned that while only evening chapel was required, there was, by the bishop's directive, a 7 A.M. Eucharist. "It would be nice if the counselors would encourage their campers to attend in a group. It could lead to some significant bonding with the campers." ("Significant" and "bonding" were two of Father Charlie's favorite words.) Then he barked, in the voice of a sergeant major, "Clergy, you'll take turns conducting the service! We'll post the schedule later today."

Since I was on for the 7 A.M. service the next morning, I suggested to my campers that it might be a good idea for us all to go together. "Besides," I added, "we've got our first softball game tomorrow. It might do us some good." That last phrase led to a knotty theological problem—or, as Father Charlie would put it, "a significant learning opportunity."

That night, back in the cabin, I stumbled into the bathroom after midnight and found ten of my twelve charges exchanging dirty jokes. My appearance triggered a panic exodus back to the bunks. When I got back to my bed, I announced, "I believe you've exchanged enough misinformation to ruin your life. Tomorrow night, after lights out, we're going to talk about sex. I'll answer any questions you have. All you have to do is write out your questions and put them under my pillow…and spelling doesn't count. Good night, gentlemen!" Now I was playing the sergeant major; I guess I caught it from Charlie.

All the softball teams had to have biblical, ecclesiastical, or theological names, although references to Lucifer or the nether world were out of bounds. So we had the Communion of Saints, Holy Apostles, Prophets, First and Second Kings, Angels, Archangels, Company of Heaven, Shadrach, Meshach and Abednego. My cabin was assigned the Gospel Bearers. Oscar from Gainesville figured out that gospel meant "good news," so our name quickly became "The Good News Bears" in honor of a current movie of similar name.

On our first day up at bat, the Good News Bears walked away with a 6-1 victory over the other sixth-grade boys' team, the First Kings. Hobart, a black kid from Jacksonville, our pitcher, had the makings of another Alex Fernandez. Stanley from Madison played first like Chris Chambliss and George from Lake City could hit like Hank Aaron.

That night in the cabin there was much rejoicing and I was ready to put my head on the pillow when Hobart asked, "What about the questions under the pillow?" There were more than a dozen pieces of paper. Some contained silly sixth-grade humor like, "How do porcupines make love?" but most, in their own awkward way, contained significant questions. I read the queries by flashlight, defining terms, translating four-letter words into something more acceptable, and providing basic information. After I read out seven or eight, they began speaking up and asking their own questions. I did my best to give them honest answers, and it was close to midnight when we called it quits.

I had not planned to get up for the early service, but was awakened by the movement of my campers around 6:30, who were dressed and making up their beds.

"What's going on?" I asked.

"We're going to church," said Stanley.

"Yeah," added Hobart. "We went to church yesterday and we won the game. Today we play the sixth-grade girls, the Angels. They have a three-run handicap, and as we discussed last night, can be very distracting. We need all of the help we can get." Under those circumstances, the least I could do was scramble into my clothes and follow the Good News Bears over to the chapel.

They beat the Angels by one run, and next day they would face the seventh-grade Apostles. The chapel scenario repeated itself the next morning and word got around the camp that the Bears had some sort of an inside track. While the Bears had the handicap this time, they didn't need it—Hobart was a wonder on the mound and Stanley handled first base like Chambliss of the New York Yankees. The raw score was 4-3. With the handicap it was 6-3. On to the Camp Weed World Series!

The Good News Bears were definitely the camp celebrities, or as Father Charlie put it, we had "bonded and become a significant group." Wherever we went in the camp, we waddled about like a gaggle of geese and were just as noisy. Arnold from Madison had called his dad, who delivered thirteen Atlanta Braves baseball caps in time for the Bears to appear on stage in the recreation hall singing their own version of "Take Me Out to the Ball Game":

Take me out to the Gulf Coast,
    Take me out to Camp Weed,
Sandspurs and 'gators and Bubba Mack,
    I don't care if I never get back!

There were verses about the food, the counselors, Father Charlie, the girl campers, fishing off the pier, cabin activities, and then the grand finale:

Take us out to the ball game,
Take us out to the crowd,
Home runs and strike-outs and double plays,
Put the Archangels into a daze!
For it's one—two—three—and you win
At the old ball game!

Everyone cheered wildly, except for the Archangels, the eighth-grade girls who had quietly managed to defeat all of their opponents, male and female. Their success was attributed in large measure to their pitcher, who was named after the Old Testament warrior-general, Deborah, and we were playing them tomorrow.

The chatter after lights-out that night was all about the game. The fact that our opponents were of the opposite sex brought out the latent male chauvinism in the group. Then we bumped into that major theological issue I mentioned earlier. Hobart noticed in the evening prayers that I didn't pray for a victory, but simply that the Bears would give it their best.

"How come you're not praying that we beat those broads?" he demanded.

"First of all, they're not broads," I lectured them. "They're girls, and the name of their team is the Archangels. They're human beings just like you and me, children of God and inheritors of the kingdom of heaven."

"Why do you think we've been getting up early every morning and going to chapel?" retorted Bubba Nelson from St. Augustine.

"What should we be praying for, then?" offered a voice from the end of the cabin.

"Why don't you tell me?" I countered, and then held my breath and prayed.

No one took the bait. The silence was terrible—or was it "significant"? Finally Bubba George offered, "Maybe we should pray for a good night's sleep?"

"That's a good place to begin," I responded. A couple of voices chimed in, "Amen." And then the chorus began, "Good night, Hobart...good night, John-boy...."

The Archangels were in the chapel when we arrived. In sharp contrast to the tough tomboy attire they had worn for the last three days, they had all fixed their hair and put on makeup and pretty dresses. "What a shrewd bit of psychological warfare," I thought.

Meanwhile, the whole camp had invaded the arts-and-crafts shop and turned it into a banner factory. Their creations were displayed all over the dining hall at lunch time, adding to the excitement that was bubbling over. "Creative tension" was Father Charlie's word for it, but by that time nobody was listening. All we wanted to know was who was going to win the game at three that afternoon.

By mutual agreement there were to be no handicaps—it was to be the Good News Bears versus the Archangels, six innings, winner take all. Hobart and Deborah were evenly matched on the mound. Their underhand pitches were fast and accurate. For three innings it was a no-hitter. Shouts of, "This is getting boring"..."Let's see some action," rippled through the crowd. Bubba George broke the ice with a home run in the bottom of the fourth inning. Unfortunately, no one was on base. A single to right field drove in a run for the Archangels and they entered the fifth tied 1-1. The boys scored two more runs in the fifth, while the girls were limited to one, bringing them into the sixth and final inning with the Bears ahead 3-2. Deborah's pitching was perfect: three batters up and three down.

Now it was Hobart's turn on the mound. If he could only repeat Deborah's performance the Bears would be the champions! The crowd was wild. "Strike three!" shouted the umpire and the first batter was retired. "Ball four" walked a player to first. A foul ball, a called strike, and a wild swing accounted for the second out. Meredith, a four-foot, eleven-and-a-half-inch blonde from Orange Park, whose earlier hits had been caught by the outfielder, was at the plate. She swung twice and missed. The third pitch was low and outside; the fourth just missed her knees and then she connected—over the center fielder and into the cabbage palms. It was all over: the Archangels' game, 4-3.

We went through the ritual of sportsmanship and cheered the winning team and they did the same for us. Deborah and Hobart shook hands and Father Charlie managed to compliment both teams without once using the word "significant."

A tired, dirty, and despondent gang of boys sat on their bunks in the cabin afterward, complaining that the umpire had made some dubious calls and rehashing the game. It was particularly embarrassing to be beaten by a bunch of girls, even if they were eighth-graders. They turned over every pitch, every swing, every possible violation of the rules, and then they turned on God.

"It just isn't fair!" said Stanley. "We went to morning chapel every day and they only went once—and he let them win!"

We chewed that line of reasoning over for another fifteen minutes until Hobart broke in: "Maybe God doesn't work that way. We're the youngest boys' cabin in the camp. We should have been eliminated the second day, but we went all the way to the top. I pitched as well as I've ever done. Maybe that's enough."

At least it was enough to get them into the shower and over to the dining hall.

For Reflection

Hear my prayer, O Lord; let my cry come to you. Do not hide your face from me in the day of my distress. Incline your ear to me; answer me speedily in the day when I call.

Psalm 102:1-2

Why do some prayers get answered and others don't? What can we expect from God, anyway? If God isn't going to answer our prayers, why bother to pray? Is praying any different from wishing?

These questions are not only part of an adolescent's crisis of faith; they are big questions for adults, too. Blowing out all the

candles on a birthday cake and expecting a wish to come true
has within it all of the elements of manipulation and magic. If
I throw a coin in the fountain, will it guarantee a certain result? Or does it take three coins?

God refuses to be manipulated. That's a tough lesson to
learn, whether you are twelve years old or pushing sixty. But
God does hear our prayers, every last one of them. Sometimes
he says "Yes" and sometimes "No." Sometimes the answer is
"Not right now" or "I have a better idea" or "There's something I want you to learn from this." I find it helpful to believe
that God knows the difference between what I want and what
I really need, and he responds to the latter.

When I was a school chaplain, the seniors enjoyed dressing
up one of their members in a clerical collar and serenading me
with, "Lord, all I want is a Mercedes Benz!" How did they
know that? God never has given me a Mercedes, but he has
provided me with reliable transportation and that was enough
to get the job done.

The real purpose of prayer, I believe, is to put me in daily relationship with God and have me open up everything to his
presence and the power of his love. I don't think that God really cares who wins a ball game, but he cares deeply about the
people who play it and the people who watch.

You might want to think about times you have been disappointed in prayer. What had you prayed for? What did you
learn when your prayer was not answered? What helped you
to begin praying again?

*And finally, when the cheering is over and the stadium empties
and darkness falls once more, be pleased to reveal in us a way
of greatness that does not require another's hurt.*

Robert Jones, from *Prayers for Puppies,
Aging Autos, Sleepless Nights*

Chapter Eighteen

Making a Difference

The only time I met Desmond Tutu we were standing face-to-face in an elevator in midtown Manhattan. Short in stature, Tutu was wearing a white cassock, purple skull cap, a pixieish grin, and he had a twinkle in his eye. He was on his way back to South Africa, but had agreed to meet with church leaders in New York, preach, hold a press conference, and answer questions over lunch.

The day was an eye-opener for me. The news media had presented Tutu primarily as a political figure, but the person I met was a man of deep spirituality and faith who always began the day with a time of quiet prayer and, whenever possible, a Eucharist. Ironically, as he told us, in his most recent exchange with P. W. Botha, President Botha had accused him of "distorting the true message of Christ" by applying it to the secular struggle against apartheid in South Africa. Much to my delight, the *New York Times* captured the theological as well as the political dimension of the story in their article, "Tutu and Botha Joust over Theology."

Over lunch, Tutu began talking about his own spiritual formation. "To belong to the church means to have people pray for you, love you, lift you up," he told us. "As Christians we belong to the community of the resurrection. We believe in a God who dies and who was raised and who lives. Therefore we believe that love is stronger than hate, justice greater than injustice, light more powerful than darkness, life stronger than death. So why worry? The worst they can do is kill you, and we belong to the community of the resurrection!"

Then he began talking about his childhood in South Africa. "I owe so much of my Christian growth to other people." Tutu told us that at the age of twelve he was confined to a tuberculosis hospital for two years, where he was visited every day by a white Anglican priest who made a great impression on him. "He always tipped his hat to my mother, who was a domestic servant, and called her ma'am."

The man was Trevor Huddleston, who had been sent to South Africa to be the headmaster of the school in Sophiatown run by the Community of the Resurrection. A former student from the school told me, "He was a gorgeous man in his black hat and white cassock. We would outrun each other to get to him. Children were always hanging on to him. He made a difference in my life. I would not be here if it had not for been for him. He helped me link my faith to fighting for justice. It was the first time that a white person ever showed affection to me. When police came in the middle of the night, he went out in his white cassock to stop them. We called him *Makhalipile,* the dauntless one."

"The dauntless one" was in his eightieth year when I spent a morning with him in London in the summer of 1992, where he was living in a modest flat over the offices of St. James's Church, Picadilly. His tall, elegant frame was only slightly stooped. The apartment was somewhat damp and chilly and he wore a long-sleeved wool sweater. His mind was sharp and his Oxford speech very clear; his eyes still had their sparkle. By then I had read all of Huddleston's books, and one phrase from the great early twentieth-century Anglican theologian Charles Gore seemed to me to run through his writing: "You have your altars. You have your tabernacles. Now it is time you found Christ in the poor and the rejected."

"I was born and bred in the strictest sect of the Pharisees: the real Anglo-Catholics of the twenties and thirties," Huddleston said when I asked him about this. An acolyte and "boat boy" at five, he entered boarding school at an early age—"I was institutionalized at seven!" Following his graduation from Christ Church, Oxford and a brief tour with his father in Ceylon and India, he was ordained a priest of the Church of England in 1937. There was no "Damascus Road" experience, no sudden conversion; the church had always played a major part in his life. "I didn't have any doubt that someday I would be ordained."

In his college years he was deeply affected by the Depression. "The hunger marchers camped out at Oxford—I was deeply moved by them and by men like Bishop Gore. It turned me into a Christian Socialist." His social concern drew him to the Community of the Resurrection, an Anglican religious order, where he took the traditional monastic vows of poverty, chastity, and obedience. Talking with his superior on the implications of this commitment, he was told, "You know the thing you're going to miss most is not having children."

"He was right," said Huddleston, but then he added that having been deprived of his own natural children, he had been given hundreds more. "Love for children became the most powerful force in my ministry." When he went to South Africa to be in charge of the mission church and school in Sophiatown, it was the children who nourished him as he cared for them. When he became Bishop of Tanzania, it was the children of that country who taught him to speak their language.

Huddleston remembers Desmond Tutu as a very frail creature whose skinny body was often racked with coughs and was not expected to live. "He was very bright and always had a lot of questions when I visited him. The doctors always said, 'Pray for Desmond. He's not going to survive.'" The old bishop was animated and excited about recent developments in South Africa that would begin to put an end to apartheid. He was especially proud of Desmond Tutu, but had no recollection of tipping his hat to his mother. "I guess that was just something I did instinctively. I was trained to tip my hat to a lady."

For Reflection

The kingdom of heaven is like a mustard seed that someone took and sowed in his field; it is the smallest of all the seeds, but when it has grown it is the greatest of shrubs and becomes a tree, so that the birds of the air come and make nests in its branches.

Matthew 13:31-32

Grace, which is another way of talking about the kingdom of heaven, is also like a mustard seed. It has small beginnings but grows into something strong and beautiful. A small gesture like the tipping of a hat is an act of courtesy. In the case of Bishop Huddleston and Desmond Tutu's mother, it was also a seed that grew into a great tree.

Later in Matthew 13, Jesus also talks about the seed that falls on good soil, takes root, is nourished, and bears much fruit. This parable of grace illuminates what happened in the life of the young boy who became Archbishop Tutu, so that as he matured he would come to see that all are created in the image of God, made for fellowship and not for division.

The architect Mies van der Rohe is credited with the statement "God is in the details," which is another way of saying that seemingly small acts of courtesy and gestures of kindness carry and convey the power of God. Huddleston had the good fortune to see the seeds he had planted grow to maturity. Not all of us are so blessed. Most of us do the best we can and pray that it is the right and loving thing to do.

You may want to recall those little events that made a difference in your life. If they were helpful, then thanksgiving is in order. If an event was harmful, then you may want to seek forgiveness. Or you may simply want to ask for God's grace to transform the chance encounter into something special, to take an ordinary moment and make it an extraordinary moment of grace.

Give us grace, O Lord, to work while it is day, fulfilling diligently and patiently whatever duty thou appointest us, doing small things in the day of small things and great labors if thou summon us to any. Go with me, and I will go; but if thou go not with me, send me not; let me hear thy voice when I follow.

Elfreda McCauley

Chapter Nineteen

"The Big One"

My wife Lynne and I were in England, vacationing on the Isle of Wight, when we heard that the first hurricane of the season was heading for our home in Miami. Earlier that Sunday morning we attended the early service at the village parish church, St. James, Yarmouth and had just completed a tour of Yarmouth Castle, an old fortress built by Henry VIII, when we received the long-distance call from Key Biscayne. It was Ken and Caroline Semon, the clergy couple from St. Louis who were occupying our apartment in exchange for conducting Sunday services in August.

I looked at my watch. It was 11:30 A.M., which meant that it was only 6:30 in the morning in Miami. "They say that the hurricane is heading right for Miami and they are ordering everybody off the island," said Caroline. "Ken's going to do the service at the church for anybody who shows up and then we're heading back to Missouri. We were going to leave on Tuesday anyway—we've been up most of the night packing the car. What do you want us to do to secure the apartment?"

"Take the furniture off the balcony and close the storm shutters," was my automatic response, but reality hadn't sunk in. Ironically, we had talked about hurricanes at length on the previous Friday when our hostess' son had driven us through the New Forest, a royal wildlife preserve near Southampton that had been hit by a freak hurricane just a few years before. He told us, "There's a hurricane blowing just five miles away from us all the time. They call it the jet stream, but if it were just a bit lower, it would be a hurricane. If we keep messing around with the ozone and all that, there's no telling just how many hurricanes we'll be having. You're about due for one in South Florida, aren't you?"

Yes, we were about due. The last one had been Hurricane Betsy, which came through in 1965 and left Key Biscayne under water for three days. Then there had been the really bad one in 1935 that took out Flagler's "Railroad Through the Sea," forever halting passenger and freight service to Key West. Originally the tracks had run right off the mainland across the water to Key West, so that you could actually board a Pullman car in Boston and wake up two days later in Cuba. The sleeping cars were transferred in Key West to a ferry boat that sailed at 10 P.M. and deposited the Pullman cars in Havana at 8:30 the next morning. The Key West extension was abandoned after it was destroyed by the hurricane, but the tracks to Miami remained a vital link between Miami and the north. With memories of these killer hurricanes still fresh in their minds, the old-timers at Vernon's Drug Store believed that Miami was long overdue for a big one and their wise advice was to get off Key Biscayne. "Take the family photo album—everything else can be replaced!"

We took the train back to London that evening, feeling helpless and powerless, although the irony was that if we were back in Key Biscayne we would have been forced to evacuate and would feel even more helpless. The BBC late news reported that the storm's name was Andrew. It had already hit the Bahamas. Four people had lost their lives and the storm was being billed as "the most powerful to target the Atlantic coast this century." It was anticipated that the storm would land on the coast between the Upper Keys and South Dade County sometime in the early morning hours. The National Hurricane Center in Coral Gables predicted winds in excess of 150 mph.

On Monday the BBC radio report simply repeated what we already knew, but added the ominous note that the equipment on top of the Hurricane Center in Coral Gables was registering winds of 168 mph when it blew away. By Wednesday morning I managed to telephone some neighbors at Island House. "Your apartment survived with minor damage, but your cars in the parking lot sure took a beating," they told us. "Key Biscayne is a mess—a tidal surge came through and flattened the state park. Trees are down everywhere in the village and none of the water and sewer lines are working."

After the early morning service on Thursday in London's St. Paul's Cathedral, a retired civil service worker, Sidney, who attended the service almost every day, asked me if I'd received any news. I told him the little I knew and added, "I just don't know what I'm going to find when I get home tomorrow." Sidney was sympathetic. He pointed to the doors of St. Paul's: "We'll be praying for you. But I want you to remember the miracle of the cathedral. If it hadn't been for the fire of London, this cathedral would never have been built. Perhaps a better Miami will come out of the ruins of the old."

On Friday afternoon our Virgin Atlantic flight landed on time at Miami International Airport. The flight attendant told us it was among the first of the international flights not to be diverted to another airport. Our senior warden was there to meet us and as we drove toward the city, things actually looked normal. "But wait until you see Key Biscayne," she warned us.

The Rickenbacker Causeway connecting the Key to the mainland was littered with boats, and large trees with massive root pads had been up-ended. A barely passable, one-lane entrance had been cut through the debris. We stopped at the Shell station to buy a case of bottled water and then walked over to the churchyard. A huge BP Oil sign had landed on the church porch just inches from the glass front. Trees were down throughout the churchyard, but a tall ghostly Australian pine, stripped of all its branches save those on its leeward side, pointed the direction of the hurricane winds.

We pushed the BP sign away from the church door and held our first service on Sunday with a better-than-average crowd for the last weekend of August. It was a thanksgiving service for our survival, for the 101st Airborne Division, which had already arrived, for the phone calls from friends and family across the country and around the world. We gave thanks for the gift of life and for the gifts of bottled water and chain saws that were already beginning to arrive from as far away as Maine and Wisconsin. Particularly touching were the gifts that came from Charleston, South Carolina: "From the survivors of Hugo to the victims of Andrew, we are praying for you, we know what you're going through." Suddenly our prayers for the homeless held new meaning. We were grateful to have a church building in which to worship, for there were many congregations in South Dade gathering under rented tents beside devastated sanctuaries.

There was no coffee hour after church that morning because the parish hall was filled with mud, but no one wanted to go home. We must have stood around for an hour after church exchanging stories of what the *Miami Herald* had called "The Big One." Let me share two of them.

Sam and Leslie Gordon spent the Saturday before Andrew hit boarding up windows and storing lawn furniture and their son's play equipment and toys in an outside shed. When the order to evacuate came on Sunday, the nearest place that could give them a reservation was a Quality Inn in Orlando. Sam piled his young family into their 1989 Volvo 740—Matthew, age two-and-a-half, Leslie, five months pregnant, and a white rabbit in a cage—and left Key Biscayne at one in the afternoon. Normally Orlando is a four-hour drive on the Florida Turnpike, but the turnpike was bumper-to-bumper traffic and by six in the evening Sam, Leslie, Matthew, and the rabbit were standing beside their broken-down station wagon somewhere north of Jupiter. They had come barely a hundred miles in five hours.

Sam located a call box. For twenty minutes he kept pushing the button for a tow truck and then he switched to the one marked highway patrol. After the Florida State Patrol car came down the grass median and radioed for a tow truck, they were pulled to a station near the Fort Pierce Interchange. Sam asked the driver if he would take a credit card. The answer was no.

"How much cash do you have?" the driver asked him.

Sam replied, "All I have is $120.00."

He took it all and disappeared. The little cash that Leslie had in her purse purchased a taxi ride to the nearest Greyhound bus station in Stuart. Busses were coming in from the north, discharging their passengers, and announcing that the trip was being terminated due to the impending hurricane in the south. The schedule posted on the bulletin board indicated an 8:30 bus scheduled for Orlando, but it soon became obvious that there would be no more busses that night.

Leslie is not certain whether she meant it as a prayer or whether she was just giving vent to her exhaustion when she said out loud, "Oh, God, won't someone give us a ride to Orlando?" At about that moment a bus driver emerged from the coffee shop. He must have heard her cry, and he said his home was in Orlando. Since his run had been canceled and there were no longer any rooms in the Stuart area, he was going to try to make it home in the bus. He offered to take the Gordons and anyone else who needed a ride.

When they arrived at the Orlando Greyhound Station, they didn't have enough money for a cab to the Quality Inn. The friendly bus driver put Sam, Leslie, and Matthew in the front of his Chevy pickup truck, but the rabbit had to ride in the back. They claimed their reservations at 11:57 that night, three minutes before the midnight deadline.

Ed Underwood, a retired attorney who had lived on Key Biscayne since 1951, remembered that Hurricane Betsy had put the entire island underwater for two days in 1965. He made reservations at the Hyatt Regency in Coral Gables long before Andrew hit the Bahamas, "just in case." On Saturday Ed and Jane Underwood, along with their daughter and little grandson, drove across the Rickenbacker Causeway heading for the mainland and their haven in Coral Gables around three o'clock on Sunday afternoon. As they crossed Biscayne Bay, there was hardly any wind and everything was normal except there were no sailboats on the water.

The Underwoods went to their rooms on the eighth floor and turned on the TV. The hurricane warnings were up for South Florida. The storm was picking up velocity and was moving in faster than predicted. By suppertime, four more members of the family had checked in from South Miami. "We had dinner sent up to the room. We really got to know our children and grandchildren." A bellboy stopped by every half hour or so to see if there was anything he could do, and periodic announcements came over the public address system. About eight o'clock the wind was beginning to howl like an express train. Looking out the window, Ed saw shingles flying by and a large sheet of copper roofing wrapped around a nearby royal palm.

Shortly before midnight there was a knock on the door; it was time to evacuate into one of the interior ballrooms. On their way down there was a loud explosive sound. A palm tree had crashed into the hotel lobby. Ed was assigned a space near the wall. He snuck out to the parking garage to check on his car, but it was like a wind tunnel out there and he was almost blown away. "To hell with the car," he said and went to find an ice machine, bringing a bucketful back to his grandchildren. He spent most of the night half-awake, listening to the hum of dozens of radios and the snores, snorts, and other assorted night noises of a hundred fellow guests.

A year later, we had a dramatic reminder of Hurricane Andrew as we tuned to the weather channel to hear the latest on Hurricane Emily. We had planned a thanksgiving service at the church that included a special gift for the victims of the midwestern flooding. A litany of thanksgiving was recited and members of the congregation were invited to share their experience of Andrew. Ed Underwood was among those who came forward.

A short, stocky man in his seventies with a bald head, he spoke gratefully and with just a touch of a South Georgia accent of his family's survival and the changes in the community since the hurricane. He also spoke of a change in his own heart.

"The Lord really laid his hand on me that night. For the first time I had a sense of what it must be like to be a refugee. I thought about the Haitians down in Guantanamo and the Krowe Avenue Refugee Camp in Homestead, and suddenly I knew what it meant to be one of them. There was no way out of the hotel and we were literally trapped for the night, but after the storm it would be all over and we would be free again. For the refugees it wouldn't be over tomorrow or next year or perhaps even in their lifetime. I thought, 'There but for the grace of God go I.' How fortunate we were and how little I had done to deserve it. God got through to me that night."

For Reflection

> God is our refuge and strength, a very present help in trouble. There-fore we will not fear, though the earth be moved, and though the mountains be toppled into the depths of the sea; though its waters rage and foam, and though the mountains tremble at its tumult. The Lord of hosts is with us; the God of Jacob is our stronghold.
>
> Psalm 46:1-4

After each of the stories in this book we ask the questions, Where do we see grace happening? In what way was God present in this situation? Were the participants aware of God's presence or grace at the time? Who or what were the agents or instruments of God's grace in this story?

It did not go unnoticed in many of the churches in Miami that on the Sunday prior to Hurricane Andrew the psalm for the day contained a description of a watery tumult, the seas that "rage and foam." A few of the hardy souls who went to church on August 23, 1992, reflected on the prophetic implications of this ancient Scripture that speaks of mountains being "toppled into the depths of the sea." What came as a great surprise to many was an unexpected discovery of God's presence in the midst of a world that was coming unglued: God's grace came through other human beings, often human beings who were previously unknown to us.

I often reflect on the fact that most of the people I know who claim to have "found God" (although I don't like that term, because God isn't lost) have found him at times of pain and trouble, not at times of victory or achievement. Could it be that when things are going well we take all of the credit, whereas when we have exhausted all of our own resources we

are then able to hear what God is trying to say to us and accept the help that has been there for us all along?

For those disruptions and disappointments that have led us to
acknowledge our dependence on you alone, we thank you, Lord.

Anne Owens,
from a Litany of Thanksgiving offered on the
first anniversary of Hurricane Andrew
at St. Christopher's by-the-Sea, Key Biscayne, Florida

Chapter Twenty

In Search of Roots

E ver since Alex Haley's best-selling *Roots* came out in the 1970s, the search for my own family roots has taken on an aura of respectability it did not have before. I used to scoff at my aunt's attempts to interest me in the family history, which I suspected was a smokescreen for recruiting my girls for the Daughters of the American Revolution. One Christmas she sent everyone a copy of the genealogical chart she had used to apply for membership in the DAR, "just in case someday the girls want to get in touch with their noble heritage." She underlined noble.

While in London one summer my curiosity got the better of me and a friend introduced me to a professional genealogist who would gladly shake the family tree for a small fee. Our initial consultation cost ten pounds. A balding man with an air of professionalism, he removed a pair of half-glasses from his vest pocket and reached for several leather-bound reference books on his library shelf. After several scholarly grunts he remarked, "I'd forget the bit about noble. With this kind of record, you'd better vote Labor."

All I knew at that point was that the original American Libby was an indentured fisherman named John who sailed out of Plymouth Harbor on November 30, 1636 and landed on Richmond Island off the coast of Maine on or about February 1, 1637. The ship, the *Hercules*, was owned by the Trelawyne family of Cornwall and Devon. In reward for his services John Libby acquired a farm on Libby River in Scarborough, Maine, near Portland. Black Point Lighthouse nearby marks the landing site: much later, Henry Wadsworth Longfellow went there to write and Winslow Homer to paint. John Libby settled down with his wife Sara and had a dozen children. A family genealogy, updated in 1993, traces all the Libbys and Libbeys back to John the Fisherman. Everybody has been assigned a number; mine is 1139364213.

My Aunt Marianne always said there would come a time in my life when the family history would become important, a kind of rite of passage. Her prediction came true quite by chance in the summer of 1984 at a Rotary Club meeting near Heathrow Airport, west of London. Waiting for the meeting to begin, a local contractor was chatting me up. When I told him my name, he said that he knew a butcher in Falmouth by that name. "Cornwall is full of Libbys. In the old days I suspect that they were all fishermen and pirates—lots of pirates and smugglers in Cornwall, and don't forget the Cornish wreckers." He told me of the bonfires they built on the cliffs overlooking the rocky Atlantic Coast. A ship approaching at night would mistake the fire for a lighthouse and crash into the rocks. Then the wreckers in their longboats would head out for the loot, clubbing to death any survivors on the way.

The train to Cornwall on the Great Western Railroad departed from Paddington Station. In about three hours we were skirting along the coast, approaching Exeter with its twin-towered cathedral, and then an hour later we were in Plymouth. I had a strong desire to get off the train, walk down to the waterfront, and imagine the *Hercules* loading up, but my ticket was to Looe-Polperro, where the telephone book indicated there was an abundance of Libbys.

We crossed the border into Cornwall on the bridge over the River Tamar, and it was evident from the names on the timetable that we were in a different country. The Cornish are Celts, related in language, custom, and dress to the Bretagnes to the east, the Welsh to the north, and the Irish to the west. They spoke a Gaelic dialect well into the eighteenth century, and the story is told that when the first Book of Common Prayer was published in 1549, the Cornish sent word to the Archbishop of Canterbury, Thomas Cranmer, that they couldn't understand the English. Cranmer wrote back, "You couldn't understand the Latin either."

At the market town of Liskeard I transferred to a narrow gauge "Toonerville Trolley" which ambled through a lush valley dropping off and picking up passengers while the sheep kept on doing what sheep always keep doing. The next day I was up at the first light and watched the fishermen head out to sea. After breakfast the innkeeper filled me in on the local points of interest as best she could and then directed me to Miss Dingle at the local museum—a helpful, straightforward person with graying hair pulled back in a bun, a tweed suit, and no-nonsense shoes—who schooled me on early seventeenth-century life in Cornwall.

"Everyone was still talking about the Spanish Armada," Miss Dingle told me. "They first sighted the ships off Looe Island, you know. The fishermen of Looe joined forces with Sir Francis Drake to defeat the invaders, and the ribs from one of the Spanish boats are in the roof of St. Martin's Church across the stream in East Looe." Looe Island is a bump of land about a mile off the coast. It has the ruins of an ancient chantry, or small prayer cottage, that was attached to the great cloister at Glastonbury. Local legend has it that Joseph of Arimathea brought the adolescent Jesus to Britain on one of his business ventures and left him on Looe Island with the monks while he went about his business, picking him up later and traveling on to Glastonbury.

Listening to these legends, I imagined young John Libby and his friends standing watch on the nearby cliffs, looking for the schools of fish that would churn the waters offshore. I could see John sitting at quayside listening to the old sailors tell of the Armada and relating tall tales of adventure on the high seas. And I could imagine a quieter John sailing his skiff out to Looe Island, tossing stones at the waves and wondering at the legends of an adolescent Christ.

My appetite for history was wetted and I have been digging ever since. My sister Ethel joined the search and together we have collected quite a bundle of information. I have also discovered that a family tree is of little interest to those outside one's own genetic cluster. Bring the topic up at a cocktail party and you'll find yourself all alone in a corner talking to a banana plant.

While I have met some interesting characters along the way, my search eventually led me to an ancient Christian community with a heritage far "nobler" than anything I could uncover by tracing a strand of my genetic code. In the fall of 1988 I stopped in Plymouth and checked into a bed and breakfast. At daybreak I stood on the Hoe, a park overlooking the harbor where Sir Francis Drake, then mayor of Plymouth, had been playing a game of bowls on July 29, 1588 when he was informed of the approaching Spanish Armada. Popular legend has it that he finished his game before tending to the invaders. I tried to visualize the Spanish ships gliding along the horizon when my eye caught sight of a small freighter leaving the inner harbor and heading into the gray Atlantic. Was it on a similar day 352 years before that my many-times-great-grandfather set sail for the New World?

Later that day, hugging the left-hand side of the road in a rented English Ford, I drove sixteen miles north on Route 386 to Tavistock, just west of the Cornwall/Devon Border. The county records office in Exeter had indicated that a John Lybbe had lived there in 1404. As the traffic arrows pointed me to the center of that market town, the most prominent landmark was the parish church of St. Eustachius, named for a second-century Roman general martyred for converting to Christianity.

Two of the church's most interesting features are the baptismal font and an ancient chest. There is a good chance that Sir Francis Drake was baptized in the font; records prior to 1614 are nonexistent, but his family did live in Tavistock and his father was the pastor of the parish. The Lybbes of Tavistock could also have splashed in those waters! The chest, discovered in 1827, contains a treasure trove of community records dating back to 1385. It was there I found out that a family with my surname had lived in the town in the fifteenth century and that in 1404 a certain John Lybbe had deeded a garden to the abbey.

The abbey....Was that where my name came from? Was John Lybbe, John-who-lived-near-the-Abbey, John L'Abbey? Maybe so. I knew I had to take a look at the abbey, or at least at what was left of it.

The ruins of the Benedictine Monastery of St. Mary and St. Rumon are adjacent to the churchyard and the two institutions had probably been part of the same complex at one time. The abbey had been founded in 974, almost a century before the Norman conquest. Like other religious communities, it had been closed down by royal edict at the time of the Reformation. Only a few crumbling walls and the outline of the floor plan of the old abbey could still be seen.

At this point I stopped wondering about my family roots and began thinking of my spiritual roots. The community begun here in 974 was part of the missionary strategy of the old Saxon church. They followed the Benedictine discipline of prayer, work, and study, gathering for corporate prayer eight times a day. They also worked hard in the community. Through their labors a nearby river was diverted into three streams that ran through the religious compound: one flushed the toilets, the second powered the mill, and the third supplied fresh water to a fish pond. Travelers sought shelter here; the sick found healing; the hungry, food; the dying, comfort. Farmers marketed their produce in stalls set against the abbey walls. What little learning was to be had was provided by catechism classes; the brightest and best went on to the university at Oxford. When the Danish raiders headed north from Plymouth, the local farmers took refuge behind the abbey walls.

What the brothers of the abbey had brought together were the building blocks of civilization. It is no wonder that the Christian faith spread like rippling waves into the countryside. Here I discovered my real roots—both my family roots and the roots I share with every Christian baptized into the household of faith. What a noble family and what a graceful heritage I had uncovered!

For Reflection

How very good and pleasant it is when kindred live together in unity!...For there the Lord ordained his blessing, life forevermore.

Psalm 133

Grace happens when people gather together in community and seek to know and serve the Lord. I'm not sure that I can really tell you what I was looking for when I started searching for my family roots. Was I looking for membership in some ancient royal household, so that I could say, "You see, I really am somebody"? Well, I found it! Grace happens in the strangest places.

The basic religious quest begins with questions like "Who am I? Where did I come from? Why am I here?" Have you ever asked yourself these questions? How have you responded? The old catechism of my church replies, "I am a child of God and an inheritor of the kingdom of heaven."

Have you ever asked yourself, "What is the purpose of my life?" I particularly like the statement in the Presbyterian catechism, "The purpose of life is to love God and to enjoy him forever."

Personally, I find it almost impossible to love and serve God without being in relationship with other Christians; this is what the Christian community is all about. What about you? Are you trying to be a Christian all by yourself? Through what communities have you received grace and support for your life in Christ?

For your presence whenever two or three have gathered together in your name, we thank you, Lord.
For making us your children by adoption and grace, and refreshing us day by day with the bread of life, we thank you, Lord.

The Book of Common Prayer

Chapter Twenty-One

The Baptism of Eric Crawford

T he first time I met Eric was at Grandma Crawford's funeral. His flamboyant style and way of dressing was in stark contrast to the ultra-conservative, button-down image of the rest of the family. That day it appeared that Eric was going out of his way to be obnoxious and to irritate the rest of the family, especially his father, Otto.

The performance was repeated two years later when Grandpa Crawford died. The old patriarch had been born in Germany. As his cancer progressed he lost command of his second language; his last words were the Lord's Prayer in his native tongue. Eric appeared at his grandfather's wake in skin-tight trousers and a white shirt unbuttoned to the navel to display the triangular gold medallion hanging from his neck on a gold chain. His black hair had been styled and sprayed; a gold earring pierced his right ear. Whenever Eric got close to his father, Otto would look the other way; his brother and sister avoided him, too. Only Eric's stepmother, Margie, made an attempt to include him in the proceedings, and she was the one who introduced us: "This is Otto's son, Eric."

Eric said he would be leaving shortly—he had a three-hour drive ahead of him and he had to get back since he was now part-owner of a "trendy hair house." But before he cut it short and dashed off, he commented, "Funerals are such prehistoric rituals. I can't imagine anything duller than Grandpa Crawford sitting up on a cloud somewhere watching all of this."

Since his father was in good health, I assumed it would be another twenty years before I ran into Eric again. Actually it was only five years later that Margie told me that Eric was in the hospital dying of AIDS and that Otto was making the six-hour trip three or four times a week to see his son. "I can't imagine what they say to each other," Margie said. "They've never been close. Otto thinks that Ronald Reagan is too liberal—Eric calls him a fascist pig!"

One Sunday after church, I asked Margie if any minister had ever visited Eric. When the answer was no, I told Margie, "Ask Otto if he would like me to visit the hospital or bring communion to Eric."

"I don't think that would work," Margie replied. "It would be a long drive for you and, besides, I don't think Eric would want it. He thinks that all clergy are pompous jerks—nothing personal," she added quickly. "He just doesn't have any use for Christianity, religion, the church, or the clergy."

"Why don't we let Eric make that decision for himself? Go ahead and ask Otto to speak to Eric anyway. If nothing else, I'd like to drive over and see him, at least—if not for Eric's sake, then for Otto's."

"Eric would probably snarl at you and throw you out of the room," she warned, "but I'll talk to Otto about it. Just don't be too disappointed if he says no."

Word came back from Otto a week later, thanking me for the offer, but declining. He had evidently talked it over with Eric's mother, who had flown in to keep vigil at the hospital. Eric's mother's reaction had been simply, "He can't take communion; he's never been baptized."

I now knew I had to talk with Eric and Otto directly, although I'm still not sure why I kept pressing the issue. Something in me wouldn't let go. I called the hospital and the ward nurse got Otto to call back collect on the pay phone. "Please tell Eric that I'd like to visit him if he's willing," I said. Then I added, "I would like to offer to baptize him. I believe he has a right to know that."

Otto didn't think that sounded very likely, but he agreed to pass my message along to his son. "What do I tell him," Otto asked, "if he wants to know what baptism is all about?"

"If you get that far with him," I answered, "let me know, and I'll come right down."

In a matter of days, I received the message that Eric did want to see me and that time was short. Otto was now staying in a motel near the hospital and spending most of his time with his son. Margie offered to drive down with me. "I can't believe that Otto is able to spend so much time with Eric" was the constant theme of Margie's conversation as we drove the interstate. The three hours went quickly.

Eric's body was wasted, his breathing labored. His dark and fearful eyes were sunk deep within his skull. Evidently he hadn't closed his eyes in three days. A good ten days' growth of beard outlined his jaw and chin. My immediate reaction was to think of a semi-abstract painting I had seen of the face of Jesus on the cross and to remember a phrase I had heard all my life, "I saw the Lord in the suffering of my brother." Eric was propped up facing the door, which opened directly onto the nursing station. At his side was a window that looked out over a lake. A massive storm cloud had darkened the afternoon sky, the kind that often breeds tornadoes.

Sitting in front of the window at Eric's bedside was his cousin, Cindy. She was twenty-something and described herself as a "very new Christian." I asked her where she went to church. She allowed that she hadn't joined one yet, but that she went to a Roman Catholic Mass on Sunday mornings and an Assembly of God prayer and praise service on Sunday nights or Wednesday evenings. Cindy told me that she felt that the Lord wanted her there. I said that it was okay with me.

I talked with Otto and he brought me up-to-date on Eric's condition. Eric didn't have much time. He hadn't slept in days. He was on oxygen and could speak only with great difficulty. Then Otto added, "I have no idea why he wants you here, but when I delivered your message about baptism, he nodded his head. Maybe it has something to do with Cindy, I don't know. But I'm glad you came."

The Baptism of Eric Crawford

Eric and I went through the formalities of being reintro-
duced. Did he know who I was? Yes. Did he remember me at
his grandparents' funerals? Yes. Had his father spoken to him
about baptism? He nodded. Did he understand what baptism
was all about? His nod this time was less than decisive, so we
read through the Bible passages appointed for the service. Eric
responded mostly with his eyes. He seemed to be listening
with great intensity when I read from the eighth chapter of
Romans, "You did not receive a spirit of slavery to fall back
into fear, but you have received a spirit of adoption."

We then went through the baptismal vows. "Do you renounce Satan and all the spiritual forces of wickedness that re-
bel against God? Do you renounce the evil powers of this
world which corrupt and destroy the creatures of God? Do
you renounce all sinful desires that draw you from the love of
God?"

Eric nodded his assent.

"Do you turn to Jesus Christ and accept him as your Savior?
Do you put your whole trust in his grace and love? Do you
promise to follow and obey him as your Lord?"

Eric's dark eyes were fixed firmly on mine. His lips silently
formed his response: "Yes."

Otto, Cindy, and Eric's nurse were witnesses. Eric's forehead was hot when I touched it three times with water, "In the
name of the Father, and of the Son, and of the Holy Spirit.
Amen."

Afterward, Otto and I joined Margie in the waiting area.
"Will you take a look at that cloud!" Margie said. It looked as if
someone had taken a knife and cut a window out of the middle of the black storm cloud. The sun was streaming through
it, creating a rainbow over the city. It was the sort of thing my
wife, who is an artist, would never dare to put in a picture.
"Too corny," she would say, "no one would believe me!"

I went back to Eric's room. Cindy met me at the door. She
asked, "Did you see the sun breaking through the cloud?" She
had adjusted the mirror over the washbasin so that Eric could
see it, too. "I told him that the Lord had opened up a door for
him. I hope that was all right."

Cindy said she planned to stay with Eric as long as necessary. We talked about Scripture passages she might read to him. High on the list was the one from Romans, "You did not receive a spirit of slavery to fall back into fear, but you have received a spirit of adoption." I also told Cindy that it would be all right if she just wanted to be quiet. "Just let him know that you're there."

Word came the next day that Eric had died early in the morning. Cindy was in the room with him. So was Otto. Cindy reported, "I had been reading to him and Eric looked at me and said that he was no longer afraid to close his eyes. I held his hand and we both went to sleep."

For Reflection

Do you not know that all of us who have been baptized into Christ Jesus were baptized into his death? Therefore we have been buried with him by baptism into death, so that, just as Christ was raised from the dead by the glory of the Father, so we too might walk in newness of life.

(Romans 6:3-4)

In the ten years that the world has been aware of AIDS, I have attended the deaths of an equal number of AIDS patients. All were male; one was married; two I baptized as infants; two I baptized on their hospital beds; some had been my students, while others were referred to me by doctors or hospice workers. In each case I did my best to offer the comfort of God's grace, whether through baptism, holy communion, the laying on of hands, or prayer.

Being attractive or deserving has nothing to do with God's grace. None of us deserve it. None of us deserve to receive baptism; none of us deserve God's love. It is God's unconditional gift to us. Baptism says it all: union with Christ in his death and resurrection, birth into God's family, the church, forgiveness of sins, new life in the Holy Spirit, and the continuing promise of God's sustaining grace.

Some of us spend seventy or eighty years or more claiming the gifts and living out the promises of our baptism. Others, like Eric, have only a few hours. In God's timetable, it doesn't matter. As I reflect on the experience of Eric's baptism, I can see God's grace at work in many areas.

The reconciliation between Otto and Eric is certainly one example of God's grace at work. The appearance of Cindy on the scene from out of nowhere is another. The intense pressure, almost compulsion, I felt to reach out to Eric and his receptivity to baptism all lead me to believe that the Lord's hand was at work putting it all together.

This might be a good point to reflect on the meaning of your own baptism and the experience of grace in your life. What were the promises that you made or were made for you at your baptism? What promises did God make to you in your baptism? Have you claimed those promises? How might things be different if you did?

Heavenly Father, we thank you that by water and the Holy Spirit you have bestowed upon your servants the forgiveness of sin, and have raised them to the new life of grace. Sustain them, O Lord, in your Holy Spirit. Give them an inquiring and discerning heart, the courage to will and to persevere, a spirit to know and to love you, and the gift of joy and wonder in all your works.

The Book of Common Prayer

Chapter Twenty-Two

Breakfast with Sterling

S cotty Stewart made a point of getting up early on Sunday morning, having breakfast at the local coffee shop, and then taking a large plastic garbage bag to pick up the trash around the church building and in the parking lot. Being a natural environmentalist, Scotty carried a second bag just for the beer cans. St. Andrew's sat across the street from a strip mall with an all-night convenience store. A disco around the corner often valet-parked cars in the church parking lot after midnight, and the trash he found the next morning left from the late-night encounters and scattered on the tarmac posed its own kind of challenge.

Scotty's Sunday routine also included a stop in the kitchen to start a pot of coffee for the minister, Sunday school teachers, choir members, ushers, and altar guild members who would soon be arriving for the first service of the day. On this Sunday he had just locked the kitchen door when, out of the corner of his eye, he spotted something unusual on the left side of the church. There was a foot attached to a human body lying flat on a concrete sidewalk that was sheltered by an overhanging roof.

Scotty's mind started to race. "It's a dead body, call 9-1-1—it's a live body, call 9-1-1—somebody got beat up in a fight, call 9-1-1—it's a drunk—no, it's just one of the street people who came in out of the rain." Scotty moved a little closer. The foot belonged to a young black man asleep on a piece of cardboard. Scotty decided to try the friendly neighbor approach.

"Good morning!" he said cheerfully. "It's time to get up."

The young man sat up suddenly and said, "I have a name, you know. It's Sterling. My name is Andrew Sterling."

"Well, Mr. Sterling, it's time to get up. There will be folks coming along this way to church in just a little while." He was about to add, "So move on out!" but Andrew Sterling was already beginning to do just that. There was no need to order him about. Scotty thought a minute and then he added, "There's a bathroom you can use just inside the door and if you'd like, I can get you a cup of coffee when you come out."

Sterling smiled and headed for the bathroom. The coffee wonder had done its work. Scotty checked the church freezer and found two ham and cheese sandwiches in the back of the "Baloney Ministry" corner. The idea behind the baloney ministry was that no one should knock at the church door and walk away hungry. Parishioners were encouraged to bring fresh sandwiches in plastic bags and put them in the freezer. (No mayonnaise or lettuce, please.) They could then be thawed out in the microwave in one minute or would be edible on their own in half an hour.

When Sterling came into the kitchen, Scotty led him out into the church garden and placed the sandwiches and coffee on a picnic table. He went back for his own coffee and then sat across from his guest. "Where are you from?"

"I'm from all over. I don't have a home."

"I mean where were you born?"

"I was born in Macon, Georgia. That was a long time ago."

"How long ago?"

"Thirty-two years."

"What kind of work do you do?"

"I paint. I do odd jobs...." Sterling paused and drank some coffee. He started to say something and then paused again. Finally he said, "I do drugs. I've got what they call a chemical dependency problem. I know I've got it, I know what it's doing to me, and I know I'm the only one who can do anything about it. It's my fault. It's not my momma's fault. It's not the white man's fault. Momma can't fix it. You can't fix it. The government can't fix it. Even Jesus can't fix it if I won't let him."

Scotty started to tell him about a drug rehab program, but Sterling cut him off. "I know that, too." Sterling stood up and took his paper plate and napkin over to the trash barrel. "That was a nice breakfast. Thank you very much."

Sterling picked up the plastic bag that contained his few belongings, looked up at the steeple for just a moment, then turned around and said to Scotty, "Please pray for me." Then he walked out to the street.

Scotty took the coffee cups back to the kitchen. He drove his car out of the parking lot just before the first usher arrived to open the church.

For Reflection

Let mutual love continue. Do not neglect to show hospitality to strangers, for by doing that some have entertained angels without knowing it.

Hebrews 13:1-2

The theme of the hidden Christ is a recurring one in Scripture and in the traditions and stories of the Christian church. The parish I serve is named for the legendary figure of St. Christopher, who unknowingly carried the Christ child across a river.

Guy de Maupassant, in his short story *A Great and Mighty Wonder*, tells the story of Conrad the shoemaker, who believed that the Christ child would visit his shop on a certain date. The day came and went, but his only visitors were a shoeless beggar, a little lost boy, and a woman selling a bundle of kindling. At prayers that night, however, it was revealed to the old cobbler that the Lord had come to him after all:

Lift up your head, for I kept my word;
Three times my shadow crossed your floor;
Three times I came to your lonely door.
For I was the beggar with bruised cold feet;
I was the woman who you gave to eat;
And I was the child on the homeless street.

In my church, candidates for baptism, when they are asked if they will commit their lives to Jesus Christ as Savior and

Lord, must also promise to respect the dignity of every human being and to serve Christ in everyone, loving their neighbors as themselves. A few chapters ago we discovered that a small gesture of courtesy on the part of one person not only turned the life of a young man to Christ, but even may have turned the whole history of a country around.

We have absolutely no idea whether anything changed in Andrew Sterling's life as a result of the chance encounter with Scotty, but we are assured that Christ was served through him. If only for a few minutes, grace happened.

Holy God, whose name is not honored where the needy are not served and the powerless are treated with contempt: may we embrace our neighbor with the same tenderness that we ourselves require; so your justice may be fulfilled in love, through Jesus Christ. Amen.

Janet Morley

Chapter Twenty-Three

The Birthday Party

W hen I was first ordained, I was assigned to the Cathedral of St. Philip in Atlanta. As the youngest priest on the staff, I spent most of my time working with teenagers, hanging out at their ball games, dances, and hamburger joints. But I took my turn at general parish duties along with the other clergy, which included taking Holy Communion to the shut-ins and people in nursing homes. "You'll have a church of your own someday," advised the dean of the cathedral, "and you need to know that there are people in this world who are over seventeen."

An organization of women called the Daughters of the King was responsible for arranging the logistics of these nursing home visits. At two o'clock sharp every Thursday afternoon, two of these women would arrive at my office, escort me to a waiting car, and whisk me away to the afternoon's appointments.

On one of my first assignments I saw an ear trumpet for the first and only time in my life. Actually it was two ear trumpets, which were attached to two ancient twin sisters whose wheelchairs were placed within inches of the portable altar where I was conducting the service. The long, slightly twisted brass horns kept getting closer as the sisters kept straining to hear. I found myself leaning over and practically yelling into the open horns.

When the service was over and we were into what was called "fellowship time," I overheard the twins yelling into each other's trumpet and realized they thought it was the Roman Catholic service.

"He's awfully young," said the one.

"Good-looking, too," replied the other.

"I understand they can't marry."

"That's a pity!"

On one afternoon I recall quite vividly, I followed the Daughters of the King out to the parking lot at exactly 2:03. We were going to visit Miss Susie, one of the senior members of the cathedral congregation. She had been baptized in the first St. Philip's, a wooden structure that had occupied a corner lot across from the state capitol. Miss Susie was a nurse who had distinguished herself during the great influenza epidemic of 1917. She was part of the little band of pioneers who during the Depression relocated the cathedral from the old downtown out to its present location in North Atlanta. One of the pillars of the church, she was a charter member of the Daughters of the King. What's more, she was turning ninety years old that very day.

Marion Siegal drove the car, and when we got to the nursing home she opened the trunk and removed a birthday cake wrapped in silver paper and crowned with a large white bow. Mary Elizabeth McGill followed with the communion silver, prayer books, and all the rest of the paraphernalia. When we arrived at Miss Susie's room, we found the birthday girl dressed for the occasion...in her birthday suit! I stepped out in the hall as Marion and Mary Elizabeth found her "something more appropriate."

Miss Susie was delighted to see us. "What have you got in that pretty box?"

"It's a birthday cake," we all said in unison.

"Oh, how wonderful!" she beamed. "Why don't you just put it on the shelf in the closet with the other one?"

"The other one?" we chorused. "What other one?"

"The one you sent me last year. It was wrapped up so pretty I had the nurses put it up there where I could look at it."

Sure enough, there it was on the shelf, hard as Stone Mountain. We explained to Miss Susie that the idea was to unwrap the cake and share it with her friends. She thought that was a splendid idea and stepped out into the hall, where she issued a general invitation. "Come to my birthday party. Y'all please come!"

And they did come, in wheelchairs and on walkers, some by themselves and some assisted by nurse's aides. They all came to the party and we had a great celebration.

Grace is like that. You have to unwrap it.

For Reflection

Someone gave a great dinner and invited many. At the time for the dinner he sent his slave to say to those who had been invited, "Come; for everything is ready now." But they all alike began to make excuses. The first said to him, "I have bought a piece of land, and I must go out and see it; please accept my regrets." Another said, "I have bought five yoke of oxen, and I am going to try them out; please accept my regrets." Another said, "I have just been married, and therefore I cannot come."

Luke 14:16-20

One of the recurring New Testament images of life in God's kingdom is that of the wedding reception, the big banquet, the wonderful party. There is only one requirement: you've got to accept the invitation. In Greek the word for grace is *charis*, which means gift. In order to use and enjoy a gift, you have to accept it. In the case of Miss Susie, she had to unwrap it and pass it around.

In Luke's parable of the great feast, many of the invited guests did not get to go to the party because they were just too busy with more important things. You might want to ask yourself how many opportunities of God's grace you have missed just because your life was so cluttered.

In Matthew's version of this story, many people don't come to the party because they don't take the invitation seriously and they respond with anger and hostility. Have you ever been angry with God? Have you ever resented the fact that he wants to get involved in your life?

Also in the Matthew passage there is a man who doesn't get to stay at the party because he wants to do things his own way. What are some of the ways you have blocked God's grace in your life because you wanted to do it your own way?

Lord God, thank you for giving the world so many gifts. Help us to receive the gifts you give us, and to use them well, even when they're not what we expect.

Susan C. Harriss, from *Jamie's Way*

Chapter Twenty-Four

Receive This Child

G retchen and her mother sat in my office. I had never seen either of them before. Gretchen was a short, stocky woman of twenty-something with a round, pretty face and a large mouth that on occasion expanded into an ear-to-ear smile. But Gretchen wasn't doing much smiling that day. She was in her fifth month of pregnancy and was beginning to show.

Gretchen had gone to see Dr. Mary Fowler, an obstetrician and a member of my congregation who was also my wife's doctor and had delivered our first grandchild. Sometimes she would come to church directly from the delivery room and present herself breathlessly at the altar rail early on a Sunday morning whispering with her contagious grin, "It was a little boy!" There was another side of Mary's practice: she performed abortions. In fact, it had become the side for which she was most known and it seemed to consume more and more of her time. Mary and I were not of the same mind regarding this matter, and we had long conversations over lunch every month or so, dialogues that would often continue with the exchange of news clippings in the hospital corridors. We didn't agree, but we liked each other and continued to talk.

Mary contended that most women arrived at her office with the decision to have an abortion already made. "You can counsel them on the alternatives, but they barely listen. They know what they want and they want to get it over with and get on with their lives. There may be 1.5 million abortions a year in the United States, but the decisions to have them performed are made one case at a time and they're usually made long before I get to talk with them."

I extended the offer that I knew at least half a dozen couples who wanted very desperately to adopt a baby. There were others in the parish who would be more than willing to take in a young woman and see her through the pregnancy and the delivery. "If you ever run into somebody who is on the fence," I told Mary, "I'll be glad to talk with her."

Gretchen chose Dr. Fowler because her office was fifteen miles away from her home. She had hoped for anonymity, since Mary had an office and not a clinic, but on her initial visit Gretchen still had to pass three picketers as she drove into the parking lot. The waiting room was a mixture of all ages and sizes. She sat by a very pregnant woman her own age whose two-year-old child kept patting her mother's stomach, saying affectionately, "Nice baby...good baby."

When Dr. Fowler confirmed the obvious and began to outline proper prenatal care, Gretchen began to cry. "I can't go through with it," she sobbed. Mary Fowler indicated that second trimester abortions could be very tricky, and that they would need to schedule the procedure as soon as possible. She was explaining the details of the procedure when Gretchen fell apart. "I can't go through with an abortion," she whimpered.

So that's how Gretchen got to my office. She was afraid of many things, but most of all she was afraid of her father's reaction to the news. "He'll be so angry he'll disown me. He'll never speak to me again. He'll probably kick me out of the house!" Her brothers posed another problem. "I'm their big sister. They look up to me. I've let them down." What about the father of the child? "He's no longer in the picture. He got nervous when I missed my first period and didn't even wait around to hear the news."

Gretchen's mother, on the other hand, supported her warmly. She preferred the idea of adoption to abortion, but she was leaving the decision up to Gretchen. She was more concerned about her husband's health than his temper, and had ruled out Gretchen's moving back into the family home with the baby for that reason. So I told Gretchen about a couple in the parish who would be willing to have her live with them until the baby was born. They had one daughter who was off at college and they had a spare bedroom. Their home was within walking distance of the local shopping mall, the hospital, and the medical pavilion.

Gretchen also wanted to know about the people I knew who wanted to adopt a baby. They were both professionals who lived in a nearby city, both in their early thirties. Stanton and Melissa had been trying to have a baby for years. They had tried every diet, read every book, made love in every possible position, and spent thousands of dollars at the local fertility clinic.

All told, we spent about three hours together. They thanked me, Gretchen flashed a grin, and they left.

It was a month later when Mary Fowler and I met for lunch at the River House and I found out what was going on. "Gretchen decided to risk telling her father. The old man didn't yell or lecture her or anything. He just wrapped his arms around his daughter and held her for a long time. She should have called you to let that couple know that she won't need their room after all. I'm supposed to get the name of your young couple and start the adoption process. Even in a private adoption all the state procedures have to be followed. I'm also having two others investigated, just in case."

Stanton and Melissa were ecstatic. I had to talk them down from their hopeful plateau. "There are other candidates. When the social workers are through interviewing all of you, they will make their recommendations and then Gretchen will make the final decision. It's a long process with no guarantees."

Three months later I had just come home from a meeting when the phone rang. It was Mary Fowler. She had just admitted Gretchen to the hospital: the baby was on the way.

The nurses let me into the labor room, which was already crowded with people. Gretchen was hooked up to all of the monitoring devices, which in turn were being monitored by her mother and four brothers. "The little fella's heart is doing 140 rpm. Isn't that a bit much for his first day?" queried one anxious young male voice. "He's just revving up his motor at the starting gate," added another uncle-to-be.

Before they moved Gretchen into the delivery room, she reached out her hand. "Please say a little prayer for me and the baby." Then she and her mother went down the hall. The cheering section and I retired to the "Father's Waiting Room." I have no idea what the other two occupants thought when they saw us come in—a priest with four young men?

Gregory arrived just before daybreak with the announcement from Dr. Fowler, "It's a little boy." The brothers and I donned green gowns, caps, and masks and were led into the nursery. We passed the baby around. Gregory was unimpressed. He had put in a hard night and wanted some sleep. We all congratulated Gretchen, said a prayer of thanksgiving, and went home. Gregory wasn't the only one who needed a nap.

When I came back that afternoon, the nurse said that Gretchen had asked for Gregory to be brought to her room so they could spend time together. She had fed the little boy and spent over an hour with him. He had just been returned to the nursery when I arrived. "Isn't he beautiful?" Gretchen was grinning from ear to ear. I sat down at the side of the bed and listened to her describe his every gesture, sound, and bodily function in minute detail. "I wish I could keep him."

"You can if you want to," I said.

"But I can't keep him. I really can't keep him. I know that. I can't give him a home. I can't give him all the things that I want him to have. Your couple can do that, can't they?"

"Gretchen, you don't have to give your baby up for adoption unless you really believe that it's the very best for him and for you."

"Tell me about your couple. Do they love each other? Do they have a nice home? Do they go to church? Will they love him?" The questions flowed. "How do I know that your couple will get the baby? How do I know that when the lawyers take him out of this room that he won't be given to someone else?"

That seemed to be the critical question. "If you don't want to place your baby for adoption, you don't have to. But if you want to be certain that 'my couple' will be the one to adopt and raise your baby, then I will deliver him personally and report back to you."

I had placed myself on an emotional roller coaster, the likes of which I had never ridden before. The next morning, after the pediatrician had pronounced Gregory fit and healthy, the attorney, a thirty-something woman, brought the legal papers to Gretchen's room. She very gently went over the documents with Gretchen, line by line. The reality of the moment began to sink in.

"Do I have to sign all of these?" Gretchen asked.

"Not unless you want to place the baby for adoption," replied the lawyer. Gretchen signed them quickly and pushed the papers away. They were witnessed by a nurse and a cleaning woman.

We walked down the hall to the nursery. They gave me a mask and draped a diaper over my shoulder. I instinctively patted Gregory for burps and checked out his diaper. Gretchen pressed her nose against the viewing window as they led me out the other side of the nursery and into an elevator. We descended in silence and walked purposefully through the hospital lobby to a large, four-door sedan. No one said a word as we drove the short distance to the offices of the law firm.

When the entrance doors swung open, I was confronted with a corridor lined with secretaries, clerks, and senior partners. A cheer went up and they all applauded. The noise startled Gregory and he opened both eyes wide, flashed a big grin, squealed, but did not cry. I was led into a back office where Stanton and Melissa had been waiting. Stanton stood up. Melissa remained seated. I placed Gregory in the arms of his new mother.

The next morning, before Gretchen checked out of the hospital, she received a bouquet of red roses along with a note, "Thank you for the gift of your son."

For Reflection

So the woman remained and nursed her son, until she had weaned him....She brought him to the house of the Lord at Shiloh....And she said, "For this child I prayed; and the Lord has granted me the petition that I made to him. Therefore I have lent him to the Lord; as long as he lives, he is given to the Lord."

1 Samuel 1:23-28

The story of the birth of Samuel the prophet is a very poignant one. Hannah, an older, barren woman who has been praying for a child, understands that the Lord is calling her to give up that child for the Lord's service. She is to place him in the hands of Eli, the priest of Shiloh. To further complicate the plot, we are told that Eli and his sons have corrupted the sanctuary at Shiloh. One can only imagine the range of emotions Hannah experienced.

And I can only imagine that the same was true of Gretchen. I can simply testify as a male observer that the giving up of her son was very painful. Grace happened, but it was not cheap grace. It was very costly. She did what she believed was the right thing for her baby and for herself, but it did not feel good at the time. She was hurting when she watched the nurse place Gregory in my arms, when she watched me walk down the hall and into the elevator. Love is a decision, not a feeling, and sometimes love cuts very deeply.

This might be a good time to reflect on the tough decisions that have been placed before you. When have you had to choose a painful course of action in order to make it possible for grace to happen?

Jesus our brother, you followed the necessary path and were broken on our behalf. May we neither cling to our pain where it is futile, nor refuse to embrace the cost when it is required of us; that in losing ourselves for your sake, we may be brought to new life.

Janet Morley

Chapter Twenty-Five

Amazing Grace

 lex Haley, the author of *Roots*, stood in the pulpit of St. Mary Woolnoth, London, and read the inscription on the church wall:

> John Newton, clerk, once an infidel and libertine, a servant of slaves in Africa, was by the rich mercy of our Lord and Savior Jesus Christ preserved, restored, pardoned, and appointed to preach the faith he had long laboured to destroy.

It was the pulpit once held by the author of "Amazing Grace," perhaps the most popular hymn in America. The organist of St. Mary's was practicing for the following Sunday and, sensing the pilgrim spirit in the visiting tourist, softly played the familiar tune. Haley sang to himself the words he had learned as a child in a black church in the American South.

> Amazing grace, how sweet the sound,
>   That saved a wretch like me!
> I once was lost, but now am found,
>   Was blind, but now I see.
>
> 'Twas grace that taught my heart to fear,
>   And grace my fears relieved;
> How precious did that grace appear,
>   The hour I first believed!
>
> The Lord has promised good to me,
>   His word my hope secures;
> He will my shield and portion be,
>   As long as life endures.

Through many dangers, toils and snares
    I have already come;
'Tis grace that brought me safe thus far,
    And grace will lead me home.

When we've been there ten thousand years,
    Bright shining as the sun;
We've no less days to sing God's praise,
    Than when we'd first begun.

Newton's life spanned most of the eighteenth century, also the time when England dominated the slave trade. His father, a ship captain involved in transporting and trading human cargo, was absent for most of his son's childhood; his mother, from whom he received his only religious training, died when he was six.

At age eleven he signed on as an apprentice sailor on his father's ship. The female slaves aboard the ship were at the mercy of the crew members and John Newton, as he grew into adolescence, was no exception—he later confessed that his behavior was "exceedingly vile." One biographer, John Pollock, notes, "It is a curious fact that there may be American or Caribbean blacks in whose veins runs the blood of John Newton."

When he was twenty Newton virtually became a slave himself for over a year in Sierra Leone, where he almost died from disease and maltreatment. Found by one of his father's ship captains, he picked up Thomas à Kempis' *Imitation of Christ* on the way home and read not only of God's grace, but of God's judgment:

> I need your grace—and I need it in great quantities to overcome nature which has been prone to evil from the beginning. Ever since nature fell and became infected by the sin of Adam, the first man, the punishments of that offence have fallen on all mankind.

Unhappy with à Kempis' message, he threw it aside. The date was March 9, 1748. That night a great storm arose. The planks on one side of the ship were shattered and the ship drew tons

of water. Newton and others bailed all night. Just before daybreak he surprised himself by shouting, "If this will not do, the
Lord have mercy on us!"

When the ship finally reached port, Newton was a changed
man. "The blasphemer was gone," he wrote later of his conversion. "I began to know there is a God that hears and answers
prayer,…though I see no reason why the Lord singled me out
for mercy." While his ship was being repaired Newton traveled to Londonderry and found lodging with a Christian family. "Twice a day I went to church. While I was there, I told the
pastor I wanted to receive the sacraments at the next opportunity.…I experienced a peace and satisfaction at the Lord's table that I had never known before."

As a result of Newton's conversion, his personal behavior
changed radically, but he still continued in the slave trade. As
captain of the *African* he cultivated his own devotional life and
conducted Anglican services for the crew on the deck, but remained almost totally oblivious to the human suffering below.
As he wrote shortly before his ordination:

> During the time I was engaged in the slave trade, I never had
> the least scruple as to its lawfulness. I was upon the whole sat-
> isfied with it as the appointment Providence had marked out
> for me. It was, indeed, accounted a genteel employment, usu-
> ally very profitable.

On his first trans-Atlantic voyage, Newton reported, nearly a
third of his 216 slaves died from disease or suicide. Their
hands and feet were chained to avoid insurrection, and they
lay as close together as "books on a shelf." "Close" meant a
space six feet long, sixteen inches wide, and five feet high.

At the age of twenty-nine Newton took a land job for medical reasons. His religious life flourished as he studied the
Scriptures, wrote hymns, and told the story of his conversion.
It was during this period that he formed a lasting friendship
with John Wesley and George Whitfield; it was probably under Wesley's guidance that he began preparing for the ordained ministry.

It was also at this time that Newton's social conscience and his sense of religious vocation began to converge. His shipboard conversion had set him on a course of personal piety, while his contact with the Wesleys opened his eyes to the evils of slavery and brought his convictions into the public sphere. Exposure to the Wesleys not only set him on an anti-slavery course, it also put him in the mainstream of the eighteenth-century renewal movement which was to define the evangelical wing of Anglicanism as well as the Methodism of his day.

In 1764 he published *An Authentic Narrative,* which gave a first-hand account of his life before becoming a Christian and established for him a national reputation. Newton's message was twofold. He never lost sight of the image of himself broken and wretched on the coast of Africa, hating God and his own soul; his constant message was of a God whose love and power was such that they could "save a wretch like me." But he also used his story as an opportunity to preach against the evils of slavery. This purpose is clear in the tract entitled *Thoughts on the African Slave Trade,* where Newton describes the dehumanizing effect on slaver as well as slave:

> A mate of a ship, in a longboat, purchased a young woman with a fine child, of about a year old, in her arms. In the night the child cried much, and disturbed his sleep. He rose up in great anger, and swore that if the child did not cease making such a noise, he would presently silence it. The child continued to cry. At length he rose up a second time, tore the child from the mother, and threw it into the sea. The child was soon silenced indeed, but it was not so easy to pacify the woman: she was too valuable to be thrown overboard, and he was obliged to bear the sound of her lamentations.

By chance—or was it providence?—an old family friend and member of Parliament sought spiritual counsel from Newton while in London, and was himself converted to Christianity. His name was William Wilberforce. At first Wilberforce wanted to become a priest like his friend, but Newton discouraged him, urging him instead to combine his considerable political skill with his new-found Christian faith: "God can make you a blessing both as a Christian and a statesman." Wilberforce said that he never spent time with his pastor without hearing him express remorse for his part in the slave trade; his relationship with Wilberforce was one step toward redeeming his past.

Wilberforce led the battle against slavery and called upon his old pastor to testify before Prime Minister William Pitt and the Privy Council appointed by King George III. The first motion in 1789 to abolish the slave trade was defeated, but, like the civil rights movement a century and a half later, the tide was going out on the old order. In March of 1807, Parliament passed Wilberforce's bill abolishing the slave trade on British ships. On December 21 of that same year, the Reverend John Newton, at the age of eighty-two, spoke his last words: "I am a great sinner and Christ is a great Savior."

For Reflection

My grace is sufficient for you.

2 Corinthians 12:9

The life of John Newton is an example of what life in grace is all about. For Newton, grace was both a moment of conversion and a lifelong process that not only altered his own personal behavior, but led him to confront the evils of his day.

In speaking of the early Christian communities, Acts 2:42 states, "They devoted themselves to the apostles' teaching and fellowship, to the breaking of bread and the prayers." In a similar way, Newton's shipboard conversion led him to seek out the company of other Christians, to receive the sacrament of Holy Communion, to study the Scriptures, and to enter upon a life of prayer. Without that response, his experience on that dark and stormy night would have been lost.

We know very little about Newton's mother except that she shared her Christian faith with her little son and that she died young. Did she plant the seeds that grew and bore much fruit? Newton's conversion was followed by a radical change in his personal life and a growing discontent with the slave trade. His friendship with Wilberforce was both the catalyst and the means for changing the system. All of these are instances of grace happening.

Newton was a man of deep personal faith and an effective agent of change in his own generation, but it did not all happen at once. It took a lifetime for both of these elements to grow into maturity. Grace for John Newton was both a moment of change and a new way of life.

One of the most controversial lines in the hymn "Amazing Grace" is the phrase, "who saved a wretch like me." It is controversial because it clashes with our basic belief that all human life, created in God's image, has infinite value. But it also touches on something deep within human experience—those times when we feel worthless. Have there been times in your life when you have felt that way? In Newton's life and in the lives of many others, such occasions are also the times when they were most ready to hear the Gospel. Can you identify moments like that in your life?

While moments of pain and wretchedness can be times of conversion or spiritual rebirth, they can also be moments when God is calling us to grow. In what areas of your life do you think God is calling you to grow? Is he nudging you to grow in your personal relationship to him, or is he challenging you to change your behavior? Is he calling you to do something about the evils in society as a whole, or is there a particular need in your community that is being ignored?

Most kind Jesus, grant me your grace so that it may be with me and work with me and remain with me to the end. Grant me this: always to desire and want what is most acceptable and pleasing to you. Let your will be mine, and let my will always follow yours and be in perfect accord with it. Let what I want always be what you want.

Thomas à Kempis

Chapter Twenty-Six

Means of Grace and Hope of Glory

Reflections on the Meaning of Grace

For most of us, grace is something you say before eating a meal. While such prayer can be a very graceful act, it does not get us to the heart of what Paul had in mind when he wrote to his friends at the church in Rome, "Grace and peace to you from the Lord Jesus Christ" (Rom. 1:7).

Let's begin by saying what grace is not. To start with, grace is not a spiritual vitamin. A friend of mine once visited a rather eccentric old lady who came to church every time the doors opened. After he complimented her for her faithfulness, she proudly produced a shoebox half-filled with communion wafers and held it out, saying, "You can never get too much of a good thing!"

Neither is grace a reward; it is not a paycheck or a bonus. It is not something we earn, deserve, or merit. In the Bible, grace has to do with God's basic attitude or disposition toward his people. There is a Hebrew word, *hen*, that is most frequently translated as "favor," meaning the kindness and graciousness shown by a superior to an inferior, especially when there is no obligation for such kindness—as when the psalmist rejoices, "By your favor, O Lord, you had established me as a strong mountain" (Ps. 30:7).

Also associated with the idea of grace in the Hebrew Scriptures is the word *hesed*, often translated as "loving-kindness." The prophet Isaiah wrote about God's grace this way:

I will recount the gracious deeds of the Lord, the praiseworthy acts of the Lord, because of all that the Lord has done for us, and the great favor to the house of Israel that he has shown them according to his mercy, according to the abundance of his steadfast love. (Isa. 63:7)

In selecting the children of Israel as his chosen people, it was God's grace, not their achievements, that was the deciding factor:

It was not because you were more numerous than any other people that the Lord set his heart on you and chose you—for you were the fewest of all peoples. It was because the Lord loved you and kept the oath that he swore to your ancestors. (Deut. 7:7-8)

Another Hebrew word, *b'rith*, is essential to our understanding not only of grace but of the entire biblical drama. *B'rith* means "covenant" and is essential to both the Old and New Testaments. It means that God has committed himself unconditionally to us human beings. In the covenant with Noah, God makes a commitment not only to Noah, but to the whole human race and all living creatures (Gen. 9:1-17). On Mount Sinai the covenant is made with Israel through Moses: "If you obey my voice and keep my covenant, you shall be my treasured possession" (Ex. 19:5). In the Christian Scriptures, Jesus speaks of a new covenant that fulfills the old; at the Last Supper Jesus says, "This cup that is poured out for you is the new covenant in my blood" (Lk. 22:20).

In the New Testament, the key Greek words for grace are *charis* and *agape*. *Charis* has at its root the idea of gift; *agape* is the word for God's unconditional love. The grace of God is fully disclosed by Christ and Christ is its complete expression:

And the Word became flesh and lived among us, and we have seen his glory, the glory as of a father's only son, full of grace and truth....From his fullness we have all received, grace upon grace. The law indeed was given through Moses; grace and truth came through Jesus Christ. (John 1:14, 16-17)

The writers of the New Testament, especially Paul, are quite clear about the fact that our relationship to God (salvation) is a free gift. It is not something we earn or deserve: "For by grace you have been saved through faith, and this is not your own doing; it is the gift of God—not the result of works, so that no one may boast" (Eph. 2:8-9). It is part of God's character to be gracious.

If I were going to single out one passage of Scripture to define grace, I would select the parable of the Prodigal Son in Luke's gospel, which is not really about sons at all, but about a father's unconditional love. Al Tuggle, who was my first senior warden at St. Christopher's-by-the-Sea, told me that when he was a young boy in South Georgia he and his buddies amused themselves by choosing up sides and throwing wads of red clay at each other. "It didn't take long for us to work our way over into a farmer's cornfield, where we discovered the great joy of throwing ears of corn at each other instead of red clay. In just a few minutes we did a lot of damage."

The farmer soon put a stop to the destruction of his cash crop by Al and his friends, and they tried to make amends. "Surprisingly enough, the farmer was very gracious and gentle with us. Harold and I and the other two boys went to the field to clean up the damaged area and straighten up the plants that were salvageable." Al still had to face his parents. The cornfield incident was dealt with; Al was forgiven.

Then the conversation took a different turn. "Now," his father said, "there is something I want to pass on to you that is important. As you go through life you can do a lot of things that will affect your mother and me. You can make us very angry, you can make us very sad, you can make us very embarrassed. There is one thing, however, you cannot do no matter how hard you try. You cannot make us stop loving you. You are our son and we will always love you, no matter what."

That promise of unconditional love is what theologians call "habitual grace," God's unending love for his whole creation. When that love reached out to the child through his father's act of forgiveness, that was actual grace. In *Wishful Thinking*, Frederick Buechner describes it this way:

A crucial eccentricity of the Christian faith is the assertion that people are saved by grace. There's nothing *you* have to do. There's nothing you *have* to do. There's nothing you have to *do*....The grace of God means something like: here is your life. You might never have been, but you *are* because the party wouldn't have been complete without you. Here is the world. Beautiful and terrible things will happen. Don't be afraid. I am with you. Nothing can ever separate us. It's for you I created the universe. I love you.

The sacraments are examples of actual grace, "outward and visible signs of inward and spiritual grace," occasions when God's love and God's presence touch our lives. In Holy Communion, the bread and the wine are the outward and visible signs of the body and blood of Christ given to his people and received by faith. Traditionally the church has set apart seven sacraments: baptism, Holy Communion, confirmation, marriage, the rite of reconciliation, the anointing with oil and laying on of hands, and holy orders. But I believe there are many more than that. There may even be as many sacraments as there are baptized Christians—maybe even more, maybe as many as there are people in the world—because God can and does use each and every one of us as instruments of his grace.

Our car had a flat tire recently on the causeway leading from Miami to Key Biscayne. To my dismay, the jack just wouldn't function properly and I exclaimed to my wife, to God, and to the passing traffic, "If I ever needed a Good Samaritan, this is the time!" Next thing I knew, a six-foot-four truck driver was standing at my side with a bumper jack to match, the answer to my prayer. I'm sure the truck driver would have dubbed me a "crazy preacher" if I had called him a sacrament, so I just thanked him and thanked God and drove my car to Tony's Citgo Station to have my tire repaired.

One of my seminary professors used to say, "It is most natural for the supernatural to use the natural." Grace happens whenever we are willing to have the Lord present in our lives, whenever we are willing to receive his love and to receive his gifts. But more often than not we get in God's way. Theologians sometimes talk about obstacles to grace, things that keep grace from happening. In the simplest of terms, the major obstacle to grace is sin. I have often defined sin as anything that separates us from God, each other, and our own true self. For the purposes of this book, I would add that sin is anything that separates us from or gets in the way of God's grace.

I once took a youth group to a neighbor's backyard for a cookout and pool party. As sometimes happens, things got a bit out of hand. Oh, I don't mean throwing the priest in the pool—that was all part of the program. But trying to see how many adolescents could fit on one aluminum chaise lounge really was over the line of acceptable behavior. The collapse came as teen number eight, Charlie, threw himself on teen number seven, Bubbles, and by the irrevocable laws of physics and gravity upon numbers one through six. There were squeals, cries, giggles, shrieks, bruises, cuts, and a torn bathing suit or two, and one piece of destroyed poolside furniture.

First we tended the sick and then we had a meeting. "What are we going to do about all this?" was the stated agenda, but the first five minutes degenerated into placing blame. Charlie's daring leap was a natural target; Bubbles's excess weight came in for some comments. Finally the eight who had actually gotten on the pile confessed to their collective sin—one actually quoted from the General Confession, "We have done those things which we ought not to have done." But what about the others who had been cheering them on and waiting their turn? It was a fascinating exercise in collective moral responsibility.

Once the group had concluded that "all had sinned," they turned their creative energy to the task of raising the money to replace the broken piece of furniture. By the time the owner of the chair returned to her house, a car wash for next Saturday had already been planned.

But the car wash never took place. Our hostess, in an attempt to be a good sport, said it really didn't matter that much. I'm sure she was trying to be gracious and forgiving, but she denied the teenagers a valuable lesson. Grace was beginning to happen in that situation as the group began to accept responsibility for its own behavior. It was a painful but creative process that was thwarted by the substitution of what could be called "cheap grace"—grace without any cost.

There is a very telling passage in the first history book of the Christian community. Right after the Feast of Pentecost, when the first Christians experienced a great outpouring of the Holy Spirit, Acts 2:42 records, "They devoted themselves to the apostles' teaching and fellowship, to the breaking of bread and the prayers." Another way to state this would be that they listened to the stories which would eventually be recorded in the New Testament, lived in community with other followers of Jesus, shared in the Eucharist, and said their prayers. In other words, the early Christians had committed themselves to live a life in grace.

Not all Christians find grace in the same place. Some find it in the word of God; others in the community of other Christians; many are nurtured by the sacraments and still others by a life of prayer. But the common thread is that they trust that God will provide them with whatever help or strength or wisdom or guidance they will need for the moment. Grace is both a moment of affirmation and acceptance by God, and a trusting relationship that goes on for a lifetime.

In all these stories, grace happened under a great variety of circumstances. And so it will always be. Grace is the buried treasure, the mustard seed, the pearl of great price, the great catch of fish.

Grace happens when we receive or accept forgiveness.

Grace happens when we reach out to someone in need.

Grace happens when an old lady picks up broken glass on the beach.

Grace happens when a slave trader in a sinking ship cries out for help.

Grace happens when a community of sisters makes a commitment to set up housekeeping in South Central Los Angeles.

Grace happens when a former hostage lets go of his hatred for his captors.

Grace happens when we say no to evil.

Grace happens when we say yes to Jesus Christ.

Grace happens when we support and encourage one another in our Christian commitment.

Grace happens when we continue in the apostles' teaching and fellowship, in the breaking of bread, and in prayer.

Grace happens when we persevere in resisting evil, and whenever we fall into sin, repent, and return to the Lord.

Grace happens when we proclaim by word and example the Good News of God in Christ.

Grace happens when we seek and serve Christ in all persons, loving our neighbors as ourselves.

Grace happens when we strive for justice and peace among all people, and respect the dignity of every human being.

Words of Grace

O n the following pages you will find additional Scripture passages, prayers, and quotations on the subject of grace from centuries of experience in the Judeo-Christian family. The common thread is that there are some things and some situations that we cannot handle by ourselves: we need God's help. That help, which is always unearned and unmerited, is called grace.

Scriptures of Grace

For the Lord God is a sun and shield; he bestows grace and honor. No good thing does the Lord withhold from those who walk uprightly.

Psalm 84:11

Toward the scorners he is scornful, but to the humble he shows grace.

Proverbs 3:34

At that time, says the Lord, I will be the God of all the families of Israel, and they shall be my people. Thus says the Lord: The people who survived the sword found grace in the wilderness.

Jeremiah 31:1-2

And the Word became flesh and lived among us, and we have seen his glory, the glory as of a Father's only son, full of grace and truth.

John 1:14

With great power the apostles gave their testimony to the resurrection of the Lord Jesus, and great grace was upon them all.

Acts 4:33

I do not count my life of any value to myself, if only I may finish my course and the ministry that I received from the Lord Jesus, to testify to the good news of God's grace.

Acts 20:24

For there is no distinction, since all have sinned and fall short of the glory of God; they are now justified by his grace as a gift, through the redemption that is in Christ Jesus.

Romans 3:22-24

My grace is sufficient for you, for power is made perfect in weakness.

2 Corinthians 12:9

For by grace you have been saved through faith, and this is not your own doing; it is the gift of God—not the result of works, so that no one may boast.

Ephesians 2:8-9

But each of us was given grace according to the measure of Christ's gift. Therefore it is said, "When he ascended on high he made captivity itself a captive; he gave gifts to his people."

Ephesians 4:7-8

You then, my child, be strong in the grace that is in Christ Jesus.

2 Timothy 2:1

For the grace of God has appeared, bringing salvation to all, training us to renounce impiety and worldly passions, and in the present age to live lives that are self-controlled, upright, and godly, while we wait for the blessed hope and manifestation of the glory of our great God and Savior, Jesus Christ.

Titus 2:11-12

Let us therefore approach the throne of grace with boldness, so that we may receive mercy and find grace to help in time of need.

Hebrews 4:16

But grow in the grace and knowledge of our Lord and Savior Jesus Christ. To him be the glory both now and to the day of eternity. Amen.

2 Peter 3:18

Prayers of Grace

O Lord our God, grant us grace to desire thee with a whole heart, so that desiring thee we may seek and find thee; and so finding thee, we may love thee; and loving thee, may hate those sins which separate us from thee, for the sake of Jesus Christ.

Anselm of Canterbury

Give us grace, Almighty Father, so to pray as to deserve to be heard, to address thee with our hearts as with our lips. Thou art everywhere present, from thee no secret can be hid. May the knowledge of this teach us to fix our thoughts on thee, with reverence and devotion, that we pray not in vain.

Jane Austen

O God, we ask thee not to lift us out of life but to prove thy power within it. We ask not for tasks more suited to our strength but for strength adequate to our tasks. Give us the vision that inspires and the grace that endures. Save us from the sin of futile sorrow which only sees but does not act. Stir up our wills to practice that brotherhood by which alone the Kingdom of the Christ is wrought on earth. And give us, we pray, the grace of Jesus Christ, who wore our flesh like a king's robe, who walked the ways of earth like a conqueror in triumph, and who now lives and reigns with thee in the unity of the same spirit, ever one God, world without end.

Stephen F. Bayne, Jr.

We bless you for our creation, preservation, and all the blessings of this life; but above all for your immeasurable love in the redemption of the world by our Lord Jesus Christ, for the means of grace, and for the hope of glory.

The Book of Common Prayer

Let us beseech him to bless us with his grace, that we may confidently call upon him, and that our prayers may be acceptable in his sight. May we be delivered from all superstition and idolatry, and truly worship him to the end, that we may look upon him as our Father and savior and he at last acknowledge us as his children.

John Calvin

156

Almighty God, you have given us grace at this time with one accord to make our common supplication to you; and you have promised through your well-beloved Son that when two or three are gathered together in his name you will be in the midst of them: Fulfill now, O Lord, our desires and petitions as may be best for us, granting us in this world knowledge of your truth, and in the age to come life everlasting.

John Chrysostom

Unto whom all hearts are open, unto whom all wills do speak, from whom no secret things are hidden, I beseech thee so to cleanse the purpose of my heart with the unutterable gift of thy grace that I may perfectly love thee, and worthily praise thee.

Author of The Cloud of Unknowing

Give us an assured hope of thy mercy and grace, that we fall into no despair through the multitude of our sins, but with faithful minds consider that for the healing of sin thou camest into the world and shed thy blood. O grant unto us free refuge and a sure defence under the shadow of thy wings and under the invincible token of thy holy cross. Receive us poor sinners which utterly trust not in any good deed or merit of our own, but only in thy mercy.

Miles Coverdale

Give us grace, O God, to dare to do the deed which we well know cries to be done. Let us not hesitate because of ease, or the words of men's mouths, or our own lives. Mighty causes are calling us—the freeing of women, the training of children, the putting down of hate and murder and poverty—all these and more. But they call with voices that mean work and sacrifice and death. Mercifully grant us, O God, the spirit of Esther, that we may say: I will go unto the King and if I perish, I perish.

W. E. B. Du Bois

As we take the thorns of life and try to work them into some kind of pattern, O God, let us not waste our energies wondering about the trouble in the world, but use them to meet it; to take it away, if that be possible; but if it be not possible, give us the grace to take up our trouble like a cross, and bear it proudly in the name of Jesus our Lord.

Theodore Parker Ferris

O Lord my God, you have created me in your own image and likeness. Grant me this grace which you have shown to be of such great importance for salvation: that I may overcome my flawed nature that draws me to sin and ruin. In my body I feel the law of sin working against the law of my mind, leading me captive to obey fallen nature in many things. I cannot resist its urgings unless I am helped by your grace, ardently poured into my heart.

Thomas à Kempis

O Father, grant us grace and help us to let thy divine will be done in us. Even if it be painful to us, do thou continue to chastise, sting, strike, and burn and whatever thou wilt, that only thy will and not ours may be done. Restrain us, dear Father, and let us not undertake nor complete anything according to our own conceit, desire, and purpose. For our will is adverse to thine. Thy will alone is good, although it does not appear so, while ours is evil, although it may seem good.

Martin Luther

Give us, Lord, the grace and power
To serve thee well each day and hour;
Grant us the zeal and fervent love
To serve as angels serve above.

Philip Melanchthon

O my God, from this world of darkness, sham, and shame, let me look in faith up to the light of thy grace; work, learn, love, by the light of thy grace; live and die in the light of thy grace; come to Mount Zion through the light of thy grace; and with an innumerable company of angels, with the spirits of just men made perfect, exult in thy light and thy grace; O my Lord and my God, both now and ever.

Eric Milner-White

O God unknown, in our mother's womb you formed us for your glory. Give us a heart to yearn for you, grace to discern you, and courage to proclaim you; through the one whom you loved before the foundation of the world, our savior Jesus Christ.

Janet Morley

O Lord our God, grant us grace to desire thee with our whole heart, that so desiring we may seek and find thee, and so finding thee may love thee, and loving thee may hate those sins from which thou hast redeemed us. I commit myself to God today. By the help of his grace, I will endeavor to keep his commandments, and to follow faithfully in the way of Jesus Christ our Lord.

Prayers for All Occasions

Help me, O Lord, to keep guard over my lips. Save me from words that hurt: from gossip and slander and lies. Let me speak only to encourage and cheer and to keep people on their feet, so that all my words may minister grace, to thy honor and glory.

Prayers for All Occasions

O God, the day returns and brings us the petty round of irritating concerns and duties. Help us to play the man, help us to perform them with laughter and kind faces, let cheerfulness abound with industry. Give us to go blithely on our business all this day, bring us to our resting beds weary and content and dishonored, and grant us in the end the gift of sleep.

Robert Louis Stevenson

O Eternal God, give me grace that I may be a careful and prudent spender of my time, so as best to prevent or resist all temptation, and be profitable to the Christian commonwealth. Take from me all slothfulness, and give me a diligent and an active spirit, and wisdom to choose my employment and fill up all the spaces of my time with actions of religion and charity; that,when the devil assaults me, he may not find me idle; for my dearest savior's sake.

Jeremy Taylor

I come, Lord; I believe, Lord; I throw myself upon your grace and mercy; I cast myself upon your blood and bowels. Do not refuse me. I have nowhere else to go: here I will stay, I will not stir from your door; on you I will trust, and rest, and venture myself. God has laid my help on you, and on you I lay my help and pardon, for life, for salvation. If I perish, I perish on your shoulders; if I sink, I sink in your vessel; if I die, I die at your door. Bid me not go away, for I will not go.

John Wesley

Quotations of Grace

We cannot know truth without grace.

Ambrose of Milan

Will is to grace as the horse is to the rider.

Augustine of Hippo

Through the golden moments of musical communion with God, Mother's words still remind me of what should come first: "Grace must always come before greatness."

Marian Anderson

Grace does not destroy nature, it perfects it.

Thomas Aquinas

When I respond to God's call, the call is God's and the response is mine; and yet the response is God's, too; for not only does he call me in his grace, but also by his grace brings the response to birth within my soul.

John Baille

As the self-offering and self-manifestation of God, revelation is the act by which in grace he reconciles man to himself by grace. As a radical teaching about God, it is also the radical assistance of God which comes to us as those who are unrighteous and unholy, and as such damned and lost. In this respect, too, the affirmation which revelation makes and presupposes of man is that he is unable to help himself either in whole or even in part.... The revelation of God in Jesus Christ maintains that our justification and sanctification, our conversion and salvation, have been brought about and achieved once and for all in Jesus Christ.

Karl Barth

God appoints our graces to be nurses to other men's weaknesses.

Henry Ward Beecher

Let grace be the beginning, grace the consummation, grace the crown.

The Venerable Bede

What is grace? Grace is God's favor towards us, unearned and undeserved; by grace God forgives our sins, enlightens our minds, stirs
our hearts, and strengthens our wills.

The Book of Common Prayer

Cheap grace is the deadly enemy of our Church. We are fighting today for costly grace....Cheap grace means the justification of sin
without the justification of the sinner.

Dietrich Bonhoeffer

I cannot talk about God or sin or grace, for example, without at the
same time talking about those parts of my own experience where
these ideas became compelling and real.

Frederick Buechner

Grace is something you can never get but only be given. There's no
way to earn it or deserve it or bring it about any more than you can
deserve the taste of raspberries and cream or earn good looks or
bring about your own birth.

Frederick Buechner

The principle of the spiritual in us is grace; its mean or condition is
faith, by which we mean the affinity, congruity, or susceptibility on
our part through which God enters into our minds and wills and becomes our knowledge and righteousness and life.

William Porcher DuBose

A man may go into the field and say his prayer and be aware of God,
or he may be in church and be aware of God; but if he is more aware
of him because he is in a quiet place, that is his own deficiency and
not due to God, who is alike present in all things and places, and is
willing to give himself so far as lies in him.

Johannes Eckhart

I have a much greater sense of my universal, exceeding dependence
on God's grace and strength, and mere good pleasure, of late than I
used formerly to have; and have experienced more of an abhorrence
of my own righteousness.

Jonathan Edwards

It's easy for us to see God's grace operating in the good, the holy, the simple, the pure things that happen to us in life. But it's not so easy to see grace operating in the pain, the ugly, the trying, and the difficult things that happen to us. Yet grace is present in all of these things.

Christopher Epting

A state of mind that sees God in everything is evidence of growth in grace and a thankful heart.

Charles G. Finney

Grace is not sought nor bought nor wrought. It is a free gift of Almighty God to needy mankind.

Billy Graham

Grace works with mercy, and especially in two properties,...which working belongs to the third person, the Holy Spirit. He works rewarding and giving. Rewarding is a gift of trust which the Lord makes to those who have labored; and giving is a courteous act which he does freely, by grace, fulfilling and surpassing all that creatures deserve.

Julian of Norwich

And in this mortal life mercy and forgiveness are the path which always leads to grace; and through the temptations and sorrows into which on our side we fall, we often are dead by the judgment of men on earth. But in the sight of God that which will be saved was never dead, and never will be.

Julian of Norwich

They travel lightly whom God's grace carries.

Thomas à Kempis

Grace is a supernatural light and a special gift of God.

Thomas à Kempis

Grace does not entirely change nature but uses nature as it finds it.

Martin Luther

If grace perfects nature it must expand all our natures into the full richness of the diversity which God intended when he made them, and heaven will display far more variety than hell. "One fold" doesn't mean "one pool." Cultivated roses and daffodils are no more alike than wild roses and daffodils.

C. S. Lewis

What the New Testament is telling us, in mysterious images and dark metaphors, is that in our life as members of Christ's body, we already are given a real but partial participation in the good things of God of which the full enjoyment awaits us in heaven. In the words of a great Christian theologian, "Grace is nothing else than a kind of beginning of glory in us."

E. L. Mascall

We cannot arrive at the perfect possession of God in this life, and that is why we are traveling in darkness. But we already possess him by grace, and therefore in that sense we have arrived and are dwelling in the light.

Thomas Merton

Take a toy away from a child and give him another, and he is satisfied. But if he is hungry, no toy will do. Thus as newborn babes, true believers desire the sincere milk of the Word. The desire for grace is, in this way, grace.

John Newton

All men who live with any degree of serenity live by some assurance of grace.

Reinhold Niebuhr

Story-writers are always talking about what makes a story "work." From my own experience in trying to make stories "work," I have discovered that what is needed is an action that is totally unexpected, yet totally believable, and I have found that, for me, this is always an action which indicates that grace has been offered.

Flannery O'Conner

The growth of grace is like the polishing of metals. There is first an opaque surface; by and by you see a spark darting out, then a strong light; till at length it sends back a perfect image of the sun that shines upon it.

Edward Payson

The existence of grace is *prima facie* evidence not only of the reality of God but also of the reality that God's will is devoted to the growth of the individual human spirit. What once seemed to be a fairy tale turns out to be the reality. We live our lives in the eye of God, and not at the periphery but at the center of his vision, his concern.

M. Scott Peck

The word "grace" in an ungracious mouth is profane.

William Shakespeare

Grace is love that cares and stoops and rescues.

John R. Stott

I am in a state of grace and if I begin to fall out of it I have only to begin to turn to find God ready to meet me.

Jeremy Taylor

The burden of life is from ourselves, its lightness from the grace of Christ and the love of God.

William Ullathorne

When desire leads to prayer...grace has entered one's life. What we thought was simply blind desire starting out on one's own, with nowhere in particular to go, turns out to be instead desire expressing a dim awareness of something already there.

Ann and Barry Ulanov

Grace is God himself, his loving energy at work within his Church and within our souls.

Evelyn Underhill

The grace of God is the good which God puts into each concrete situation over and above all that man can do or plan or even imagine.

Henry Nelson Wieman

We should know the grace of the Gospel to be so certain and ready, and trust it, so that we may establish our hearts in no other doctrine.

Ulrich Zwingli

C owley Publications is a ministry of the Society of St. John the Evangelist, a religious community for men in the Episcopal Church. Emerging from the Society's tradition of prayer, theological reflection, and diversity of mission, the press is centered in the rich heritage of the Anglican Communion.

Cowley Publications seeks to provide books, audio cassettes, and other resources for the ongoing theological exploration and spiritual development of the Episcopal Church and others in the body of Christ. To this end, it is dedicated to developing a new generation of theological writers, encouraging them to produce timely, creative, and stimulating publications of excellence, and making these publications available widely, reaching both clergy and lay persons.